EXPERIENCES OF CRIME ACROSS THE WORLD

Experiences of Crime across the World

Key findings from the 1989 International Crime Survey

Jan J.M. van Dijk, *The Hague*
Pat Mayhew, *London*
Martin Killias, *Lausanne*

Kluwer Law and Taxation Publishers

Deventer ● Boston

Kluwer Law and Taxation Publishers
P.O. Box 23   Tel.: 31-5700-47261
7400 GA Deventer   Telex: 49295
The Netherlands   Fax: 31-5700-22244

Cover design: Eset

ISBN 90 6544 463 7

Contents

Chapter 1: Introduction   1
Purpose of the survey   1
Background   2
The Working Group   3
Participating countries   4
Details of the survey   5
     Sample sizes   6
     Fieldwork   6
     Computer assisted telephone interviewing   6
     Survey companies   7
     Sampling   8
     Response rates   8
     Weighting   9
     Statistical significance   9
Coverage of the questionnaire   9
Outline of the report   10

Chapter 2: Victimization rates   13
Introduction   13
Theft of cars   15
Theft from cars   16
Vandalism to cars   19
Theft of motorcycles/mopeds/scooters   20
Theft of bicycles   21
Household burglary (with entry)   23
     House type and burglary risks   24
     Reporting patterns and insurance   25
Attempted burglary   26
Robbery   27
Other theft of personal property   28
Sexual incidents   32
Assaults/threats   35
Overall patterns of victimization   39
     Incidence victimization rates   42
Victimization rates in Warsaw (Poland)
and Surabaja (Indonesia)   43
     Methodological aspects   43
     Results   43
A preliminary analysis of international differences   45
     General findings   45
     Urbanization   46
     Vehicle ownership   47

Opportunity and vehicle theft   49
Bicycle theft and car theft   52
Victimization rates and police recorded crime   53

Chapter 3: Offences and victims   **59**
Place of crime   59
Victim characteristics   60
  Gender differences   61
  Going out   61
  Independent risk factors   62
  High income as a risk factor   63
  Within country results   64
  Gender, victimization and employment   65
Overall patterns of reporting to the police   67
  Reasons for not reporting   69
Satisfaction with the police on reporting   70
General satisfaction with the police   71
Victim assistance   72
  Assistance received   72
  Interest in victim support   74

Chapter 4: Responses to crime   **77**
Fear of crime   77
  Street crime   77
  Burglary   79
Attitudes to punishment   81
  Public opinion and imprisonment rates   83
  Community service orders   84

Chapter 5: Crime prevention measures   **85**
Crime prevention   85
  Caretakers   85
  Burglar alarms   87
  Lighting   89
  Surveillance by neighbours   91
Insurance   93
Gun ownership   94

Chapter 6: Summary and conclusions   **95**
Summary   96
Discussion   103
  Telephone ownership   104
  Response rates   105
  Comparison with other indicators   105
  Police figures   106
  Independent surveys   106
  Other comparative studies   107
The future   108

Chapter 7: Summaries in French and German   **111**
    Resumé   111
    Zusammenfassung   122

Annex A: Survey methods   **133**
    Fieldwork execution   133
    Telephone penetration   134
    Telephone sampling methods   135
    Response information   137
    Face-to-face interviewing in N.Ireland and Spain   140
Annex B: Weighting procedure   **145**
Annex C: Statistical significance   **151**
Annex D: The International Victimization Survey Questionnaire   **153**
Annex E: Additional tables   **173**
References   **183**

Acknowledgments

The international survey, of which the main findings are reported here, has in all stages been a joint venture of many different organizations and individuals. We want first of all to thank the Research and Documentation Centre of the Ministry of Justice of the Netherlands for its overall funding and administrative support. We also want to express our appreciation of the other ministries and national research centres who accepted our invitation to join this rather adventurous undertaking.

In all participating countries we have been aided by national experts who were involved in the preparation and translation of the questionnaire and in the execution of the fieldwork. Without their continuous support, the survey could never have been carried out.

We are greatly indebted to Aad van der Veen of Inter/View (Amsterdam, the Netherlands) who supervised the preparation of the computer-programmed questionnaires and the performance of the subcontracted local firms.

We are indebted, also, to a circle of colleagues from various countries who generously offered us their help and advice. Of these we want to mention in particular Wesley Skogan, Ron Clarke, Francesco Pascual Mayol and Jozef Sahetapy.

We want to thank Sjaak Essers, Monique Overwater, Iris Passchier, Margreet Slis and Rebecca Lawrence for their invaluable help with the data analysis and preparation of the manuscript.

1 Introduction

Purpose of the survey

The international victimization survey reported here measured experience of crime and a number of other crime-related issues in a large number of European and non-European countries. It used tightly standardized methods as regards the sampling procedure, method of interview, questions asked, and analysis of the data. By asking respondents directly about a range of offences that they had experienced over a given time period, the survey provides a measure of the level of crime in different countries that is independent of the conventional one of offences recorded by the police. The police measure has well-known limitations for comparative purposes as it is based only on those crimes which are reported to the police by victims, and which are recorded by the police.

The value of the survey is that it:
- enables individual countries to see how they are faring in comparison with others in relation to crime levels;
- provides some rough picture of the extent to which survey-measured crime in different countries matches the picture from figures of offences recorded by the police;
- provides some basis for explaining major differences in crime experience in terms, for instance, of socio-demographic variables;
- allows some examination of the types of people most at risk of victimization for different types of crime, and whether these vary across the jurisdictions in the survey; and, finally,
- provides information on responses to crime in different countries, such as opinions about the police, appropriate sentences, fear of crime, and the use of various crime prevention measures.

These survey results should not be seen as giving a definitive picture of crime, and responses to it in different countries. The samples of respondents interviewed in each country were relatively small, only those with a telephone at home were interviewed, and response rates were not always high. The significance of these factors is taken up in more detail in the final chapter, but the fact remains that the comparable information provided by the international survey is unique.

1

Although the study serves mainly descriptive purposes, some results about victimization risks are interpreted within the perspective of criminal opportunities theory (Mayhew, Clarke et al., 1976; Cohen, Felson, 1978; Van Dijk, Steinmetz, 1984).

Background

There has long been a need for comparable information about levels and patterns of criminal victimization in different countries. Researchers have principally wanted to test theories about the social causes of crime by means of cross-national comparisons. Policymakers have principally wanted to understand better their national crime problems by putting these in an international perspective. To date, by far the major effort has been put into analyzing crime rates in different countries on the basis of offences recorded by the police (hereafter 'police statistics'). Compilations of these statistics by the United Nations and Interpol, for instance, have often been used, even though they tend to be incomplete, marred by language difficulties, and often restricted to unhelpfully broad crime categories.[1]

More critically, however, police statistics have substantial limitations for comparative purposes. First, reports of crime by victims form the major bulk of incidents that the police have available to record; any differences in the propensity to report to the police in different countries will seriously jeopardise comparisons, and rather little is known about these differences.[2] Second, comparisons of police statistics are severely undermined by differences in culture and law, and by technical factors to do with how offences are classified, defined and counted. Even within a single country, research has confirmed that different police agencies can 'count' crime differently; at national level the differences can only be greater.

In many countries recently, an alternative count of crime has been obtained through victimization (or 'crime') surveys. These ask representative samples of the population about selected offences they have experienced over a given time, whether or not they have reported them to the police. Typically, such surveys also gather information on what 'typical' offences are like, and ask respondents' opinions about crime, fear of crime, and so on. They have done much to elucidate the 'truer' level and nature of crime, the extent of unrecorded offences for different crime categories, and in particular the

---

1. For a history of attempts to make comparisons see, eg, Neuman and Berger (1988). Many studies have been restricted to developed countries and to selected crime types, while some studies look not at levels and patterns in criminality, but at the relationship between crime and socio-economic factors. Kalish (1988) presents one recent comparison of levels and trends for a range of countries reporting to Interpol, with additional information on homicide from WHO statistics.

2. Skogan (1984) has examined reporting crime to the police from data in some national and local surveys. He shows reasons for *not reporting* to be broadly similar, with seriousness of the incident a major factor. Few firm conclusions could be drawn about levels of reporting because of differences in survey design.

distribution of risks across different groups - upon which police figures generally say rather little.[3] However, by no means all countries have conducted such surveys, and those that have done so have used different methods which make their results extremely difficult to use for comparative research. Differences in the basis of sampling, method of interview, coverage of offences, and procedures for classifying offences etc, all influence the number and types of crimes counted.[4]

The case for a standardized survey in different countries has been clear to many. A proposal by the OECD in the early 1970s resulted in some pilot work in the United States, the Netherlands and Finland (Tornudd, 1982), but thereafter the initiative flagged. The idea of different countries funding an international polling agency to add victimization questions to ongoing polls has never been seen as attractive, perhaps because of doubts about how criminologically informed such a venture would be.[5]

The Working Group

The climate ripened for a standardized international survey as more was understood about the methodology of crime surveys, and the value of their information. At a meeting in Barcelona of the Standing Conference of Local and Regional Authorities of the Council of Europe at the end of 1987, Jan van Dijk formally aired plans for a standardized survey (Van Dijk et al., 1987). The momentum was continued through a Working Group comprising Jan van Dijk (overall coordinator), Ministry of Justice, the Netherlands; Pat Mayhew, Research and Planning Unit, Home Office, England; and Martin

---

3. See Skogan's (1986) discussion of technical aspects of victim surveys; Block's (1984a) collection of studies for a useful review of the features of various surveys; Sparks's (1982) comprehensive assessment of their origins and value; Mayhew (1985) for a review of major findings, and Gottfredson (1986) for another coverage of these, albeit from a North American perspective.
4. The best comparisons can be made with surveys designed to be similar, though these have been restricted in country coverage. For example, Mayhew and Smith (1985) looked at results from the 1982 British Crime Survey, which was conducted in England and Wales and Scotland. Comparisons have also been done of surveys carried out since the early 1970s in the Scandinavian countries (eg, Sveri, 1982). A similar questionnaire was used in postal surveys about crime in Texas (USA), Baden-Württemberg (W.Germany) and Hungary (Teske, Arnold, 1982). With independently mounted surveys, data need to be directly manipulated to improve consistency. Access to data is one problem, but even with access some differences cannot be accounted for. Some comparisons which have standardised design differences are taken up in Chapter 6. Avoiding the problems of comparing victimization levels, some work recently has instead assessed whether *patterns* of victimization are the same from selected surveys. For instance, Van Dijk and Steinmetz (1983) have considered the relationship between 'lifestyle' factors and crime on the basis of the Greater Vancouver and Dutch surveys. Comparisons of the British Crime Survey and the US National Crime Survey have been done by, eg, Maxfield (1987), Sampson and Wooldredge (1987), and Sampson (1987). See also Block (1984a).
5. On its own initiative, Gallup included some victimization questions in polls in 1984, though there were substantial comparability problems, and unhelpful offence definitions (Gallup International, 1984).

Killias, University of Lausanne, Switzerland. The Working Group accepted responsibility for the questionnaire, appointing the survey company, issuing invitations, and preparing the preliminary report on results which is presented here.[6]

Participating countries

A formal invitation to join in the survey was sent to some twenty-odd countries. Fourteen countries eventually took part in a fully co-ordinated survey exercise, each appointing a survey coordinator to liaise with the Working Group. The countries and their sponsors were:
- Australia (Australian Institute of Criminology)
- Belgium (Ministry of Justice)
- Canada (Department of Justice, Research and Development)
- England and Wales (Home Office)
- Federal Republic of Germany (Bundeskriminalamt, Max-Planck Institut)
- Finland (National Research Institute for Legal Policy)
- France (Ministry of Justice)
- The Netherlands (Ministry of Justice)
- Northern Ireland (Northern Ireland Office)
- Norway (Ministry of Justice)
- Scotland (Scottish Home and Health Department)
- Spain (Ministry of Justice)
- Switzerland (l'Office Federal de la Justice)
- USA (US Department of Justice)

In addition, local surveys using the same questionnaire were conducted in *Poland* (Ministry of Justice), *Indonesia* (Guru Besar Kriminologi, Penologi, Victimologi dan Hukum Pidana, Surabaja), and *Japan* (National Research Institute of Police Science; Japan Urban Security Research Institute). The fieldwork in these three countries was organized independently from the Working Group. This report concentrates on results from the fourteen full participants, with an occasional reference to results from the local surveys in Warsaw (Poland) and Surabaja (Indonesia). Data from Japan were not available for inclusion at the time of preparing this report.

It can be seen from the list of full participants that the survey does not give complete European coverage: notable exceptions are Sweden, Denmark, Austria, Italy, Portugal and Greece. Nonetheless, its coverage is extensive

---

6. Although the Working Group has had overall responsibility for the questionnaire, drafts were commented upon by a number of criminologists experienced in crime surveys, including: Wesley Skogan, Richard Block and Ron Clarke (USA); Jacques Van Kerckvoorde (Belgium); Kauko Aromaa (Finland); Carl Steinmetz (The Netherlands); Renee Zauberman (France); Irvin Waller (Canada); Helmut Kury (FRG); Helen Reeves and Joanna Shapland (England); and Juli Sabate and Francesco Pascual (Spain).

within Europe, and there is a very useful non-European perspective (from the USA, Canada, and Australia).

Details of the survey

The present survey has many features of other independently organized crime surveys with respect to the types of crime it covers, and how well it measures these. It is based on only a sample of the population, so that results are subject to sampling error, which is a limitation especially for the more rare types of offences. (Sampling error is taken up again below.) The survey is confined to counting crime against clearly identifiable individuals, excluding children. (Crime surveys cannot easily cover organizational victims, or victimless crimes such as drug abuse.) Even discounting crime unreported to the police, the survey will take a broader and probably more value-free count of incidents than police statistics, which filter incidents which *could* be punished, and which the police regard *should* occupy the attention of the criminal justice system. In many ways, however, this broader count of crime is itself a strength of the survey.

As against this, it is likely judging by methodological work, that the survey will provide an *undercount* of the extent of crime. Adequate representation of the population is always problematic in sample surveys, and those who are and who are not contacted may differ from each other - a point returned to. It is also well established that respondents fail to report in interview all relevant incidents in the 'recall period'; that they 'telescope in' incidents outside this period and that they may under-report various offences, for instance involving people they know, and sexual offences. There is also evidence that certain groups (eg, the better educated) are more adept at answering victimization questions, and that thresholds for defining deviant behaviour as criminal can differ across groups. There is little way of knowing how far these response biases are constant across county. The tendency to forget more trivial incidents may, for instance, be a relatively universal phenomenon, and some types of differential 'response productivity' may also be constant. Nonetheless, it cannot be ruled out that respondents *as a whole* in different countries will have different views as to what constitutes criminal victimizations against them, and this should be borne in mind.

It should also be remembered that the results of the present survey are only at country level. Crime risks and even attitudes to crime may vary as much between jurisdictions within countries as between countries themselves.

The major features of how the international survey was conducted are described below. Fuller details of fieldwork execution, etc. are given in Annex A.

5

Sample sizes

To encourage as full participation as possible, it was clear that the survey should be relatively modest in cost terms, affecting sample sizes and length of interview. Most countries were thought unlikely to be able to afford a large sample and on the basis of preliminary costings, the Working Group recommended 2,000 interviews.[7] Most countries opted for this, though there were smaller samples in Switzerland (1000), France (1502), Norway (1009), Finland (1000) and a larger one (5274) in W.Germany. Samples of this size, of course, produce relatively large sampling error, and restrict the scope for detailed analysis of issues on which a small proportion of the sample would have provided information.

Fieldwork

Fieldwork in most countries started in January 1989 and lasted six to seven weeks (see Table A.1, Annex A). Fieldwork in a few countries (Spain, N.Ireland and the USA) started somewhat later. An average interview lasted about 10-15 minutes depending mainly on the extent of victimization experience reported.

Computer assisted telephone interviewing

Cost was one consideration in deciding to interview by telephone, using the technique of computer assisted telephone interviewing (CATI) - a relatively new technology. More important, however, was the scope for much tighter standardization of questionnaire administration. The merits of CATI are considerable. It allows all interviewers to work with the same questionnaire on which routing is identically programmed. This itself produces fewer mistakes and errors in filtering patterns since interviewers have to enter an in-range response for each question before they can move on. CATI also allows a sample to be drawn which is geographically unclustered, and based on full coverage of telephone owners, including those with unlisted numbers. Telephone interviewing provides good opportunities to contact respondents who are often away from home since selected telephone numbers can be called at different times at no great cost. Two minor disadvantages are seen as the inability to edit the completed interview and correct mistakes (though these should be few); and loss of face-to-face contact which prevents the interviewer from seeing that a respondent is confused and does not understand the question.

---

7. The costings per 1,000 respondents were 23,000 ECU's on average in the European countries (app. 14,000 pounds sterling, 45,000 German marks and 150,000 French francs) and around 33,000 US dollars elsewhere. The costings of samples of 2,000 were 30 per cent higher.

Telephone interviewing, and in some instances CATI, has been used for some time in victimization surveys in Canada, the Netherlands, Switzerland, and the USA, for example. Methodological work has shown that, in general, victimization counts from telephone interviews are similar to those obtained in face-to-face ones. In a comparison of interviewing methods used in victimization surveys in several countries, Killias et al. (1987) concluded that the problems that arise when people are interviewed about crime depend less on the survey method used (eg, face-to-face interviews, CATI, or mail questionnaires) than on the efforts made to secure high-quality fieldwork.[8]

It was acknowledged that those with a telephone in the home might differ from those without. However, in all 12 countries where only CATI was used at the very least 70% had telephones, and in most countries the figure was nearly 90% or higher. In Spain, telephone penetration was much less than 70% outside urban areas. Thus, most interviews in non-urban areas were conducted by face-to-face personal interview (58% of all interviews); most interviews in urban areas were conducted through CATI (42% of all interviews). In N.Ireland, where national telephone penetration was estimated to be under 70%, all interviews were personal. Details of telephone penetration are shown in Table A.2 in Annex A.

Annex A discusses in more detail whether any bias has been introduced into the results on account of interviewing mainly those with telephones. Briefly, it is argued there that the present results may not be greatly distorted on this account. Telephone ownership does not relate to the experience of different crimes in any consistent way, and there is no evidence to suggest that victimization counts are lower than if fuller representation of the population had been possible. Because of this it was considered inappropriate to weight the data to take account of differential telephone ownership.

Survey companies

Inter/View (the Netherlands) were appointed as the contractor for the survey as they had experience of using CATI internationally on social science topics and indeed were probably the only company then able to mount surveys on the scale needed (Burke Source, 1987). Fieldwork was sub-contracted by Inter/View to companies abroad - often their own subsidiaries. Each participating country took out a contract with Inter/View, who prepared the

---

8. Some other earlier assessments which showed little difference in victimization counts were Catlin and Murray (1979) in Canada and Klecka and Tuchfarber (1978) and Roman and Silver (1982) in the USA. In contrast, a study by Woltman et al. (1980), concluded the number of reported victimizations were less when telephone interviews were used as the major mode. Very recent work (McGinn, 1989) is now suggesting that since the US National Crime Survey switched from ordinary telephone interviewing to CATI at the beginning of 1987 for a proportion of its sample, CATI is increasing the number of victimizations that respondents are reporting - for reasons which are as yet unclear.

computer-programmed questionnaires in different languages, and had technical responsibility for the performance of the sub-contracted local firms. Piloting of the questionnaire was done in English, French, German, Dutch and Finnish (see Annex A).

Sampling

Telephone number sampling frames differ somewhat across county, and precise techniques for sampling differed a little on this account (details are given in Annex A). However, in all countries using CATI, a regionally well-spread selection of households was sampled with some variant of random digit dialling techniques. Within each household contacted by telephone, a procedure was used to select randomly a respondent of 16 years of age or older, based on the composition of the household. No substitution of the selected respondent was allowed. Face-to-face interviews applied standard national quota sampling procedures; this was because of the considerable cost savings over other methods of probability sampling which strictly give a more representative population sample.

Response rates

Response rates were variable, and in some cases rather low. In the 13 countries using CATI, the average response rate was 41% (ie, completed interviews with the household members selected for interview out of 100 eligible households that were successfully contacted.) In four countries response rates of over 60% were achieved, while in seven the level was less than 45%. Response rates in some countries may have been lower than was expected due to the rapid growth of telephone interviewing which has reduced people's willingness to respond to surveys over the phone; low response in W.Germany and the USA in particular may partly have been influenced by this. The sensitivity of crime as a survey topic may also have played a part, as well as increasing awareness of data protection - though in some countries these factors seemed to pose no problem. There is some suggestion that good response was positively related to high telephone penetration, though there are notable exceptions to this (eg. W.Germany and the USA).

The question of whether the results from the survey have been influenced by the variable, and sometimes low response rates is addressed in full in Annex A. Briefly, the issue is a complex one, and few firm conclusions can be drawn as to the size and direction of any bias that might have occurred. The fact that the evidence is equivocal suggests the bias may not be substantial. Uncertainty as to how response rates affect estimates made it inappropriate to consider any weighting of the data to account for differential response.

8

When people did complete an interview, their response to it was reasonable. The victimization questions themselves appeared to cause respondents less concern than those on crime prevention habits (eg, use of a burglars alarms and locking behaviour). A proportion of respondents phoned the police or survey coordinators to check the credentials of the survey, though the numbers varied somewhat by country.[9]

Weighting

Results presented throughout this report are based on data which have been weighted to make the samples as representative as possible of actual national populations aged 16 or more in terms of gender, regional population distribution, age, and household composition (see Annex B for more details). Current international statistics on variables such as income, tenure or urbanization were too inadequate to allow further weighting in these terms. These variables however were collected in the survey itself and analysis by them is possible. As said, there is no satisfactory information available on which weighting for differential telephone ownership could have been made.

Statistical significance

The statistical significance of differences between the various national victimization rates and other key findings can be determined on the basis of the nomogram given in Annex C.[10]

Coverage of the questionnaire

Eleven main forms of victimization were covered as shown below. For three crimes, sub-divisions are possible.

Household property crimes
- theft of car

---

9. Each country was asked to ensure that someone was available during the fieldwork period to deal with enquiries from respondents. The interview started with a preamble explaining local sponsorship of the survey, and emphasising that it was an international exercise. In all countries instructions were given to coordinators to make sure that respondents were given the opportunity before continuing to telephone them or administrative personnel in the survey company for further details.
10. With samples of 2,000 and an overall victimization rate of say 5%, deviations of more than 1% will be statistically significant at the 95% level. For an overall victimization rate of, say 1%, deviations of 0.5% would be significant. When the sample is 1,000 (of women only for example), deviations from an overall average of 5% of more than 1.4% will be significant, and with an average of 1% deviations of 0.7%. When the overall average is about 50%, with a sample of 2,000, deviations of 2.2% will be significant. Strictly, sampling error should take into account the fact that data has been weighted.

- theft from cars
- vandalism to cars
- theft of motorcycles/mopeds/scooters
- theft of bicycles
- burglary
- attempted burglary

Personal crimes
- robbery
- theft of personal property
  . pickpocketing
  . non-contact personal thefts
- sexual incidents
  . sexual assaults
  . offensive behaviour
- assaults/threats
  . assaults with force
  . threats without force

Respondents who had been victimized were asked short questions about the place where the offence occurred; its material consequences; whether the police were involved (and if not why not); satisfaction with the police response; and any victim assistance given. In addition, some basic socio-demographic and lifestyle data were collected. Some other questions were asked about: fear of crime; satisfaction with local policing; crime prevention behaviour; and the preferred sentence for a 21-year old recidivist burglar.

Outline of the report

This report is intended to give an overview of the key findings of the survey. In-depth analysis is continuing and more details of the full range of data in the survey will be available in due course.

Chapter 2 presents, by country, rates of victimization in 1988 and over the past five years for crimes covered in the survey. The findings of the local surveys in Warsaw (Poland) and Surabaja (East Java/Indonesia) are reported on separately. For most types of crime, some additional information on the nature of the victimizations is presented, albeit not all that is available from the survey. At the end of Chapter 2, the relationship between some global social and economic characteristics of the countries and victimization risks are taken up, and how vehicle ownership rates relate to risks of vehicle crime. Comparisons for some types of crime are also made between survey victimization rates and police statistics of recorded offences.

Chapter 3 presents some comparative data on the distribution of risks of victimization in terms of age, gender, size of place of residence, income and lifestyle. Some attention is also paid to differences in rates of reporting crime to the police, and reasons for not reporting. Also dealt with is how satisfied victims who did report were with the police response, as well as satisfaction with local policing among respondents generally. Attitudes towards special victim assistance programmes are also covered.

Chapter 4 deals with survey results about the public's fear of street crime and burglary; it also looks at sentences that those in different countries said they would prefer for a 21-year old recidivist burglar.

Chapter 5 presents some key findings from a set of questions about precautions taken against household crime, particularly burglary. A short word is also said about insurance coverage, and gun ownership levels.

A summary of main results is presented in Chapter 6. Some points are also returned to about the scope and reliability of the present study.

2 Victimization rates

Introduction

Respondents in the survey were asked to relate incidents of crime which had happened to them over the last five years. This fairly long 'recall period' was taken to increase the number of victims and offences identified so that more could be said about them. Those who replied affirmatively were subsequently asked whether the incident had taken place in 1988 ("last year"), earlier than this, or in 1989. If respondents had been victimized in 1988, they were asked how many times it had happened: once, twice, etc - up to five times or more.

Rates of victimization are reported below for both the 5-year and the 1988 period. Various details of what had taken place were collected in the survey, and some of this information is discussed. For those who had experienced more than one incident of a particular type, the details related to the last incident that had occurred. The percentages of different offences which were reported to the police, for instance, are based on information given about the last incident of the type experienced over the 5-year period.

Rates of victimization can be expressed in various ways. Most rates presented in this report are *personal prevalence* rates: ie. the percentage of those aged 16 or more who experienced a specific form of crime once or more. (For example, 16.6% of all Australians had a burglar enter their home at least once over the past five years, and 4.4% had this experience in 1988). *Incidence rates* are a common alternative. These express the number of individual crimes experienced by the sample as a whole, counting *all* incidents against victims. For example, in 1988 there were 5.7 burglaries per 100 Australians, a higher rate than the 4.4% prevalence rate because some people would have been burgled more than once.

Unlike incidence rates, prevalence rates - the main rates used - do not allow any calculation, frequently made in national surveys, of the overall number of crimes committed in a country (derived by multiplying estimates for the survey population up to the total population). However, with the present sample sizes this would be hazardous. Neither are prevalence rates sensitive to differential proneness to multiple victimization. There is further work that can be done on this, but country rankings for all crimes are very similar whether incidence or prevalence rates are used.[1]

Personal prevalence rates, then, are considered to reflect accurately how many of the population are afflicted by crime, either individually or as a member of a household. In terms of respective levels of crime in different countries, 1988 and 5-year figures give a very similar picture.[2] On the basis of past studies, however, findings about the last year (1988) will be most accurate, because less serious incidents which took place longer ago than a year tend to be forgotten by some respondents. This memory loss explains the finding that victimization rates over five years are much less than five times as high as the 1988 rate: they are on average in the region of three times higher.[3]

In order to facilitate international comparisons, the tables and graphs following show a grand total rate for the fourteen countries combined, as well as individual country rates. The overall total rates are based on figures which treats each country as being of equal statistical importance, with an assumed sample of 2,000. This is so that results from countries with the largest samples do not bias overall figures. Where the total rate for Europe is presented, this has been calculated by means of weighting individual country results according to population size. (If this had been done for the overall total rate, it would have biased results too much in the direction of large countries such as the USA.)

The figures on which most of the main graphs in the rest of this chapter are based, are shown in Annex E. Table E.1 shows 1988 prevalence rates; Table E.2 shows 5-year prevalence rates; Table E.3 shows 1988 incidence rates; and Table E.4 the percentages of incidents reported to the police.

----

1. In calculating incidence rates, offences occurring 'five times or more' were counted as five. The correlation between country positions as measured by prevalence and incidence rates in 1988 for all offences taken together is very close ($r=0.934$, $n=14$, $p<0.01$). Figure 26, later in the chapter, shows details of overall incidence rates. For individual offences, the correlations between incidence and prevalence measures are all high (greater than 0.9).
   In these, and many other comparisons like them in this report, Spearman's rank order correlations are used, as these are most appropriate with the number of cases involved. When a high positive correlation is referred to it means that the ranking of the country on one variable (eg, prevalence rates for all crimes) is similar to its ranking on another (eg, incidence rates for all crimes). Correlations are based on the main 14 participating countries, unless otherwise specified. Correlations of 0.456 will be statistically significant at the 5% level: ie, there is less than one chance in twenty that the finding is due to sampling error.
2. The correlations between 5-year and 1988 victimization rates were all very high, and statistically significant at the 1% level.
3. Five-year victimization rates are higher than 1988 rates by a factor of 3.82 times for burglary with entry, down to 2.51 times for car vandalism. Five-year rates are lowest for offence categories which will include more minor incidents - eg, car vandalism, sexual incidents (including instances of offensive behaviour), and assaults/threats. These are more likely to be forgotten over a long recall period.

National victimization rates for offences against vehicles (theft of and from cars, car vandalism, theft of motorcycles, and theft of bicycles) will be partly determined by the distribution of ownership, and this issue is taken up at the end of the chapter. For the moment, prevalence rates for offences involving vehicles are calculated on the basis of the total population sample in each country, as they are for other crimes.

Theft of cars

The interview opened with an inventory of the motor vehicles and bicycles owned by the respondents' household. Next the question was put to car owners whether any of the households' cars (including trucks and vans) had been stolen in the past five years. As explained, one of the follow-up questions was, whether the theft had taken place last year (in 1988) or longer ago. Figure 1 shows 5-year and 1988 prevalence rates for car theft.

Figure 1: Victimization rates for car theft. Percentage victimized in the past five years and 1988

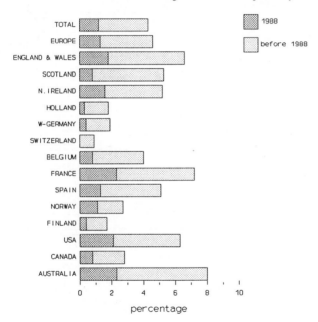

The 1988 victimization rates for car theft varies from zero in Switzerland to 2.3% in France and Australia. The 5-year rates were similarly ranked, being highest for Australia (8.0%), France (7.3%), England & Wales (6.6%) and the USA (6.3%).

15

In all countries, the majority of car thefts had taken place near the respondent's own home or in the local area, though 16% of victims in W.Germany and 9% in Belgium had cars stolen abroad.

Three-quarters of all stolen cars were eventually recovered in most countries. The results suggest that the recovery rate may be somewhat lower in W.Germany (56%), Belgium (61%) and the Netherlands (67%).

In all countries, virtually all car thefts were reported to the police (see Figure 2). The reporting percentages, as said, relate to the last incident mentioned of any that the respondent had recalled for the last five years (see table E.4 for reporting rates in 1988 and in past five years).

Figure 2: Percentage of car thefts reported to the police

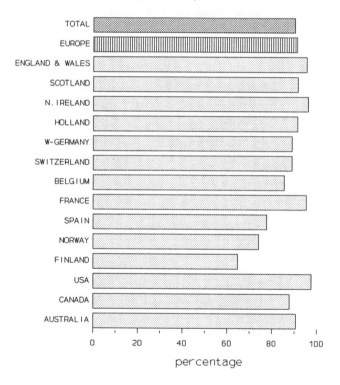

Theft from cars

The second form of crime asked about was theft from a car, covering both items left in the car and parts taken off the car, such as a wing mirrors, badges etc. The prevalence of theft from a car in 1988 was highest in Spain

16

(9.9%), the USA (9.3%), Canada (7.2%) and Australia (6.9%). Much lower rates were found in Switzerland (1.9%), Belgium (2.7%), Finland (2.7%), and Norway (2.8%). Five-year figures showed a similar picture, with risks in France also relatively high. Details are shown in Figure 3.

Figure 3: Victimization rates for theft from a car. Percentage victimized in the past five years and 1988

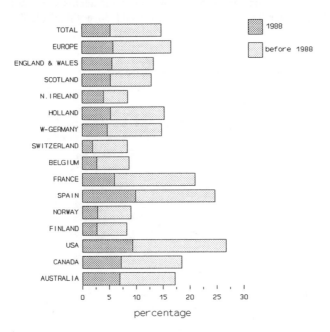

In most countries, thefts from cars were committed near home (about 50% were) or elsewhere in the city or local area (about 30%). Offences happening abroad were commoner in countries with lower risks. A full 41% of incidents involving the Swiss were committed outside their country, 17% among Belgians, 11% among Finns and 10% among W.Germans. Risks for these countries, therefore, exaggerate the amount of theft from vehicles for which residents were responsible.

The mean estimated value of the stolen property, including repair costs, was 400 ECU's (or about 500 US dollars).[4] The estimated values were higher in W.Germany, Switzerland, Norway, France and the USA and somewhat lower in England & Wales and Scotland.[5]

The percentage of thefts from cars reported to the police varied between 32% in Spain to 83% in W.Germany (see Figure 4). Rather low reporting rates were also found in N.Ireland and Australia (55%). The reasons for not reporting thefts from cars were mostly that the incidents were "not serious enough" (average 44%), that the "police could do nothing" (19%), or that the "police won't do anything about it" (14%).

Figure 4: Percentage of thefts from cars reported to the police

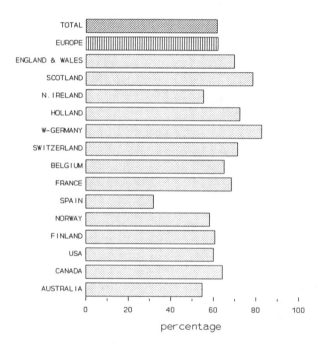

percentage

---

4. On account of some problems with the Belgium data such as a very high number of "don't know" answers, these have been excluded in this preliminary analysis. This applies to all data about financial costs in the survey. By way of illustration, there is one ECU to 1.19 US dollars, 1.36 pounds sterling, 2.03 DM and 6.93 French francs.
5. A comparison of the medians shows the same ranking.

18

Vandalism to cars

The victimization rate for vandalism (malicious damage) to cars in 1988 was highest in Canada (9.8% of respondents reported vandalism), the USA (8.9%), Australia (8.7%), W.Germany (8.7%), and the Netherlands (8.2%). Relatively low rates were found in Finland (4.0%), Switzerland (4.1%), N.Ireland (4.5%) and Norway (4.6%). On 5-year figures, the picture was fairly similar. Figure 5 shows details.

Figure 5: Victimization rates for car vandalism. Percentage victimized in the past five years and in 1988

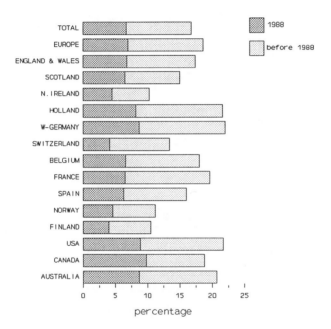

In all countries, the majority of incidents of car vandalism were committed near home (approximately 50%), or elsewhere in the city or local area (about 33%) - a very similar pattern to thefts from cars. In Australia these percentages were 34% and 58% respectively.

The mean value of the estimated damage was 300 ECU's (or about 350 US dollars). The estimated values were again relatively high in France, Switzerland, Norway, the USA and W.Germany.

Reporting car vandalism to the police was relatively uncommon in general. The average for all countries was that 39% of incidents were reported, varying between 22% in Spain, 25% in Australia, and 56% in the USA (see Figure 6). The reasons for not reporting were mostly that the incident was "not serious enough" (average 47%), that the "police could do nothing" (25%) or that the "police won't do anything" (10%).

Figure 6: Percentage of incidents of car vandalism reported to the police

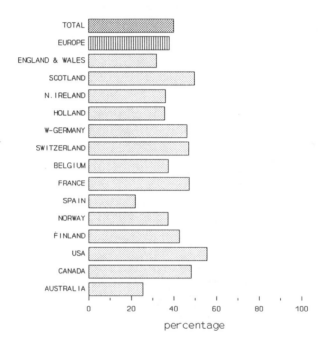

Theft of motorcycles/mopeds/scooters

With the exception of Switzerland (1.2%), less than 1% of respondents in all countries reported in the interview that they had experienced a theft of a motorcycle (motorcycle/moped/scooter) in 1988 (Figure 7). However, ownership of motorcycles varied considerably, so that the victimization rates for owners which are discussed later are more informative.

Figure 7: Victimization rates for motorcycle theft. Percentage victimized in the past five years and in 1988

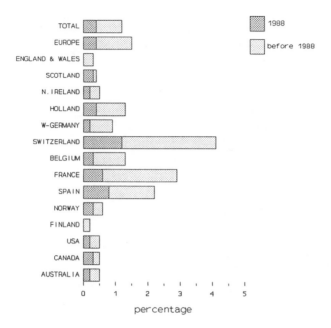

The numbers of motorcycle thefts described were too small to allow comparisons of secondary information. The overall findings indicate that half of the vehicles were recovered and that 80% of the thefts were reported to the police.

Theft of bicycles

The 1988 prevalence rate for bicycle theft was by far the highest in the Netherlands (7.6% of respondents reported a theft). It was particularly low in Spain (1.0%), England & Wales (1.0%) and Scotland (1.0%). Over five years, those in the Netherlands were again much more at risk (24.8% of people had experienced a bicycle theft). Figure 8 shows details.

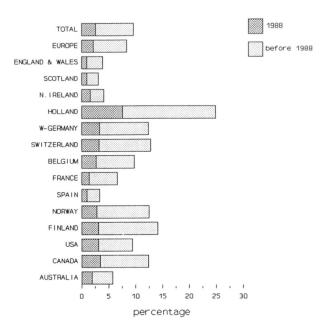

Figure 8: Victimization rates for theft of bicycle. Percentage victimized in the past five years and in 1988

Bicycles were typically stolen near home or elsewhere in the city or local area. About a quarter of all stolen bicycles were recovered - though Switzerland had a much higher recovery rate of 67% (N=128).

On average, two-thirds of bicycle thefts were reported to the police (see Figure 9). The results indicate that reporting was somewhat lower in Spain (27%) and Norway (45%). It was fairly high in the Netherlands, a country with an extremely high prevalence rate. The main reasons for non-reporting were that the incident was "not serious enough" (36%), that the victim "solved it himself" (11%), that the "police could do nothing" (19%) and that the "police won't do anything" (14%). A large minority mentioned "other reasons" (21%); this possibly indicates that the bicycle was recovered soon after the theft.

Figure 9: Percentage of stolen bicycles reported to the police

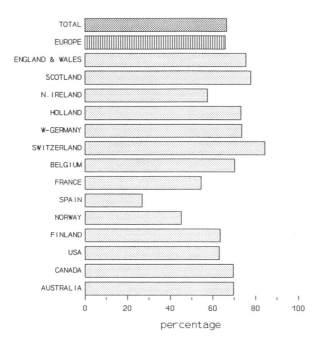

Household burglary (with entry)

The survey had two measures of burglary: (i) incidents in which a burglar entered the home ('burglary with entry'); and (ii) incidents of attempted burglary. (Detailed information about the incidents were collected only for burglaries with entry.) The 1988 victimization rates for burglary with entry were highest in the non-European countries, Australia (4.4%), USA (3.8%) and Canada (3.0%). In Europe, both the 1988 and the 5-year prevalence rates were relatively high in France, England & Wales, Scotland and the Netherlands. Low rates were found in Finland, Norway, and Switzerland (see Figure 10).

In 18% of the burglaries nothing was actually stolen. The mean estimated value of the stolen property was 1,600 ECU's (or about 1,900 US dollar). The estimated values were relatively high in W.Germany, Norway, the USA and Australia.

In 45% of cases there was damage done as well. The mean cost of the damage done was estimated at 250 ECU's (300 US dollar). These costs were also relatively high in W.Germany and Norway.

23

Figure 10: Victimization rates for burglary with entry. Percentage victimized in the past five years and in 1988

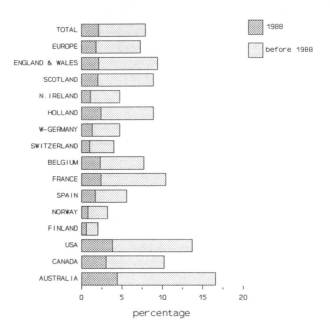

House type and burglary risks

Combining data from all countries, burglary rates differed by type of dwelling, and this was so regardless of the size of the place of residence. Boats and caravans were at highest risk (13.1% were burgled over the 5-year period). Semi-detached/detached houses had risks of 8.6%, terraced houses of 7.0%, and flats/maisonettes also of 7.0%.

Burglary risks were not consistently related to the distribution of housing types within individual countries: ie, different types of dwelling varied in their vulnerability to burglary according to country. In the USA burglary risks were by far the highest for flats (19.2%; detached houses 11.4%). Risks for flats were also relatively high in England & Wales, N.Ireland, France and Finland. In Australia, however, burglary risks were the highest for detached houses (24.5%; flats 15.8%). This was also true for W.Germany and Switzerland. In Scotland, the Netherlands, Belgium and Spain terraced houses had the highest burglary risks. In Canada and Norway burglary risks did not clearly differentiate according to house type at all. These differences are no doubt, for one, because of different housing patterns. In some countries, for instance, flats may usually be located in higher-risk urban

24

locations, and on this account will be more vulnerable; in other countries, flats will be a common type of housing for a broader range of households.

The high burglary risks in Australia may possibly be related to the fact that a great number of Australian houses are detached or semi-detached (85%). Generally, however, there was no clear relationship between the percentages detached houses and flats per country and national burglary rates.

Reporting patterns and insurance

Most burglaries with entry were reported to the police in all countries (average 81%). The exception is Spain (47%) which may be because of the relatively low proportion of households who had insurance cover against burglary. Figure 11 shows details. In general, those who said they had no insurance cover against burglary were less likely to report to the police (65%) than others (88%). Similarly, countries with a relatively low proportion of households with insurance cover have generally lower reporting rates for burglary (r=.604).

Figure 11: Percentage of burglaries reported to the police

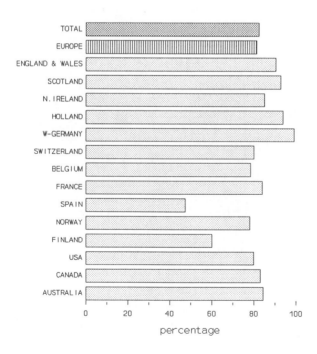

percentage

Attempted burglary

Respondents also reported on attempted burglaries, as evidenced by damage to locks/doors or windows or scratches around the lock. Attempts seemed relatively common in the USA, Australia and Canada, as was the case with burglaries with entry (Figure 12). Risks were also relatively high in the Netherlands, France, and Belgium. They were not especially so in England & Wales and Scotland, where risks of burglaries with entry had emerged as relatively high.

Risks for attempted burglary did not clearly differentiate according to housetype (boats, caravans: 15.5%; semi-detached/detached: 6.8%; terraced: 6.0%; flats: 7.0%). If risks for attempted burglary are compared with risks for burglary with entry, burglaries in semi-detached/detached houses and terraced houses appear to be somewhat more often successful than those in boats/caravans or flats (the percentages successful burglaries are 56% for semi-detached/detached, 54% for terraced houses, 50% for flats and 46% for boats/caravans). The differences, however, are too small to draw definite conclusions.

Figure 12: Victimization rates for attempted burglary. Percentage victimized in the past five years and in 1988

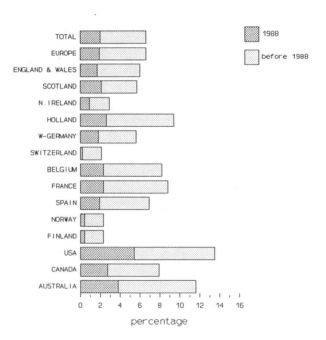

Robbery

The 1988 victimization rates for robbery (theft with force) were highest in Spain (2.8%) and the USA (1.9%). In most countries, the 1988 rate was below 1%. The 5-year rate was relatively high in Spain, the USA and Belgium (see Figure 13).

Figure 13: Victimization rates for robbery. Percentage victimized in the past five years and in 1988

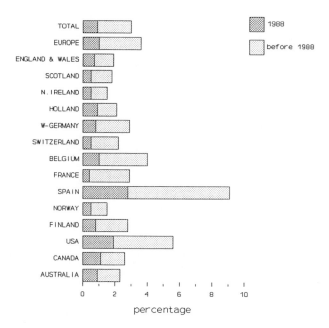

Robberies usually took place near home (36%) or elsewhere in the city or local area (42%). Although the numbers of victims do not allow definite conclusions, the findings indicate that Swiss, German, and Finnish citizens were relatively often victimized abroad.

In half of the incidents described in the survey, offenders used no weapon during the robbery, though 20% had a knife, and 8% a gun. The sharpest deviations to this pattern were that in Spain 40% of incidents involved knives, and in the USA 28% involved a gun. Chapter 5 looks at national ownerships rates for guns.

In fourty percent of the cases, nothing was actually stolen from the victim by the offender. This finding indicates that in a great many cases robberies

27

are unsuccesful. The mean estimated value of the stolen property was 250 ECU's (or about 300 US dollar).

Rather more than four out of ten robberies were reported to the police on average (Figure 14). Consistent with the more frequent use of guns in the USA, a relatively high percentage of robberies were reported to the police (58%), though there were higher figures in England & Wales (68%), and N.Ireland (60%). In Spain the reporting rate was significantly lower (30%) than elsewhere, despite the fairly frequent use of knives. Reporting was also low in Norway (33%) and Finland (32%). The major reason for non-reporting was that the incident "was not serious enough".

Figure 14: Percentage of robberies reported to the police

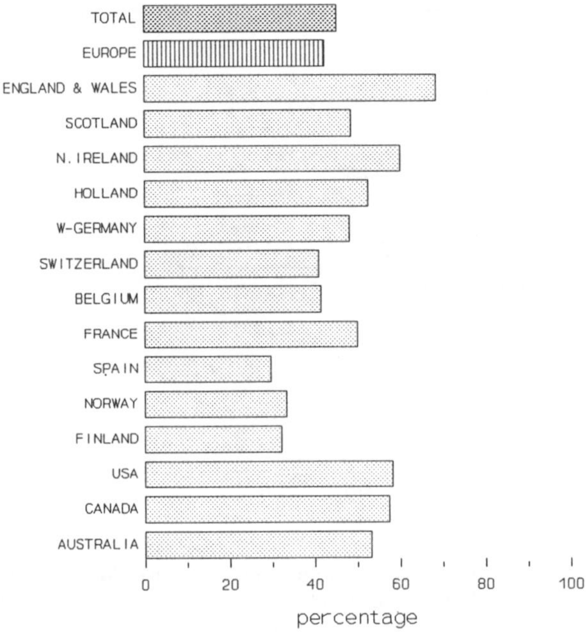

Other theft of personal property

The questionnaire gathered information about other types of theft of personal property (such as pickpocketing, or the theft of a purse, wallet, clothing, jewellery, sports equipment at work, at school, or in a pub or the street). Victimization rates for personal thefts were less variable across the participating countries than for other types of crime, though this conceals a rather different pattern for one category of such thefts - pickpocketing. The 1988 victimization rates were highest in Canada (5.4%), Spain (5.0%) and Australia (5.0%). The 5-year rates were relatively high in Switzerland (15.9%), Belgium (14.9%), Australia (14.6%), the Netherlands (14.3%), and the USA (14.2%). Figure 15 shows details.

The mean estimated value of the property stolen was 200 ECU's (or about 250 USA dollar). The estimated values were relatively high in W.Germany, Switzerland, Norway and the USA.

There is a strong suggestion in these and other data about costs that the value of the stolen property and/or damage done, is the highest in countries with the highest Gross Domestic Product per capita, such as the USA, Switzerland, Norway and W.Germany.[6]

Figure 15: Victimization rates for other personal thefts. Percentage victimized in the past five years and in 1988

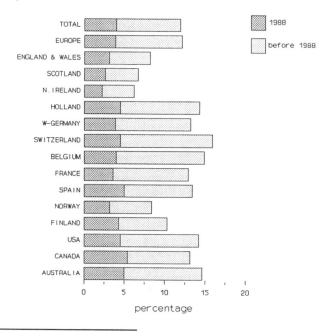

6. Countries were rank ordered according to the total mean value of the property stolen in cases of personal theft and according to GDP per capita (Euromonitor, 87). The Spearman's correlation coefficient was .497 (n=12). Since reliable data on the value of stolen/damaged property and/or GNP were not available for Belgium and N.Ireland, these countries were excluded from the analysis. The GNP per capita of Scotland was estimated to be lower than that of England & Wales but higher than that of Spain. The correlation was weakened by Finland, a country with a moderately high GNP but low values of stolen/damaged property. This may be a result of sampling error, since the number of victims in the Finnish sample was rather low.

Most thefts of personal property involved no contact between victim and offender.[7] But in roughly a third (35%) of all cases the victim had been carrying or holding what was stolen (pickpocketing). The percentages of thefts which involved pickpocketing were significantly higher in Spain (52%) and France (50%) and lower in Norway (27%). Pickpocketings were lower in the USA (24%), Canada (15%) and Australia (17%) than in Western Europe generally.

Figure 16 shows estimated risks of pickpocketing and other, non-contact thefts in 1988.[8] Rates for pickpocketing were highest in Spain (2.8%), France (2.0%), the Netherlands (1.9%), Switzerland (1.7%) and Belgium (1.6%). Low rates were found in Norway (0.5%), N.Ireland (0.9%), Scotland (1%) and Australia (1%). Australia, the USA (1.3%) and Canada (1.3%) rank lower on pickpocketing than they do for other crimes.

---

7. The main question about thefts of personal property had as a subsidiary whether or not the respondent was holding or carrying what was stolen. This information was collected only for the last incident which had occurred over the full five-year recall period.

8. Rates of pickpocketing in 1988 are based on the subset of respondents for whom the 'last incident' fell in 1988. The rates were calculated as follows. First the number of respondents were calculated whose last incident in 1988 was a case of pickpocketing. Next we estimated the number of double victims whose last incident was not a case of pickpocketing but whose first incident was, by applying the overall percentage of pickpocketing cases to all those whose last case was not pickpocketing. In roughly the same fashion, the number of pickpocketing victims among triple and other multiple victims were estimated. These estimated numbers were added to the original numbers, in order to estimate the prevalence rate of pickpocketing. The same procedure is applied to sexual assaults as a subset of sexual incidents, and assaults with force as a subset of assaults/threats.
Some respondents have been victim of both pickpocketing and non-contact theft. They are counted as victims of pickpocketing. As a consequence, the rates for personal thefts other than pickpocketing given in Figure 16 are slightly lower than the actual rates. This also applies to rates for offensive sexual behaviour and for threats without force presented in figures 19 and 22.

Figure 16: Victimization rates for pickpocketing and other, non-contact personal thefts. Percentage victimized in 1988

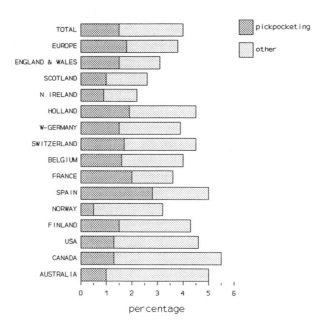

Almost three-quarters of thefts of personal property took place near home (average 24%) or elsewhere in the city or local area (50%). About 9% of the thefts had been committed abroad. Victimizations abroad were, again, particularly frequent among Swiss (21%) and Finnish (24%) victims.

On average somewhat less than half the cases of personal theft were reported to the police (see Figure 17). Major reasons for non-reporting were that the incident was "not serious enough" (38%), that it had been "reported to other authorities" (11%), and that the "police could do nothing" (21%).

Of the cases of pickpocketing 50.2% were reported to the police on average, which is only slightly higher than the rate for non-contact personal thefts.

Figure 17: Percentage of personal thefts reported to the police

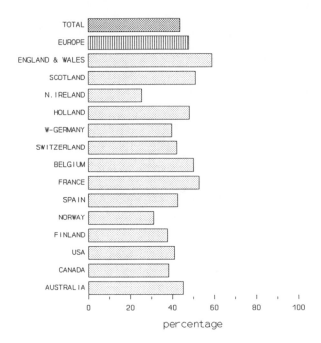

Sexual incidents

The question which was put to respondents to examine their experience of sexual crimes and offensive sexual behaviour was as follows:

"People sometimes grab or touch others for sexual reasons in a really offensive way. This can happen either inside one's house or elsewhere, for instance in a pub, the street, at school or at one's workplace. Over the past five years has anyone done this to you. Please take your time to think about it."

Measuring sexual offences in surveys is clearly difficult, and because in pilot work reading this question to men appeared to cause some problems, it was put to female respondents only. Even so, the findings must be interpreted with care, since both the readiness to answer such rather intimate questions and the definitions of offensive acts may differ between countries. In most countries (though the USA was an exception), victimization rates were significantly higher among women with a high level of education, and this may indicate a higher sensitivity to such acts amongst this group.

32

The question asked allows two types of sexual incidents to be distinguished: (i) sexual assaults (rape, attempted rape, and indecent assaults); and (ii) offensive sexual behaviour. Taking the two together first (Figure 18), women outside Europe were most likely to have been subject to sexual incidents (or be sensitive to them, or prepared to admit them). In Australia, 7.3% of women reported sexual incidents in 1988, 4.5% in the USA, and 4% in Canada. In Europe, relatively high rates were found in W.Germany (2.8%), the Netherlands (2.6%), and Spain (2.4%).

Figure 18: Victimization rates among women for sexual incidents. Percentage victimized in the past five years and in 1988

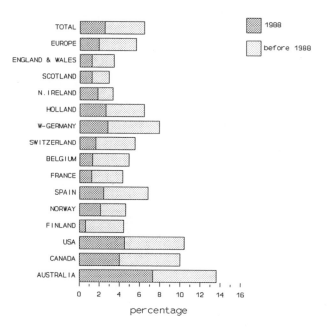

Of the incidents described, 3% were defined as actual rapes, 9% as attempted rapes, 17% as indecent assaults, and 69% as "offensive behaviour" (5 year recall period). Of all incidents, 29% can be described as sexual assaults. Women in Finland (50%), Scotland (48%), Belgium (43%) and W.Germany (40%) were particularly likely to say the incidents they experienced were assaults.

Figure 19 shows separately 1988 risks among women of sexual assaults and offensive behaviour. As explained before, these risks are estimated on the basis of information about the last incident (see footnote 8). Rates for sexual assaults were highest in the USA (2.3%), Canada (1.7%), Australia

(1.6%) and W.Germany (1.5%). There was a fairly close relationship between the two types of sexual incidents: women in countries reporting relatively many instances of offensive behaviour also reported relatively many assaults (r=0.477).

Figure 19: Victimization rates for women for sexual assaults and offensive behaviour. Percentage victimized in 1988

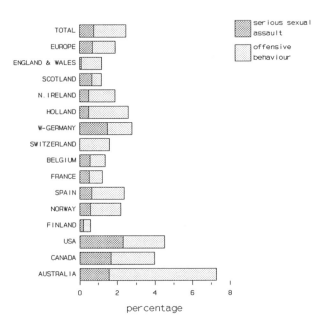

A much larger proportion of victims of sexual incidents reported multiple incidents in 1988 than victims of any other type of crime: 42% reported more than one incident, and 15% reported having been victimized five times or more.

Overall, a third of the victims knew their offenders by name and another 15% by sight. The proportion of victims in Scotland (52%) and Canada (52%) who reported knowing their offender by name was significantly higher than average (33%), and in Spain (12%) and Switzerland (11%) significantly lower. These secondary findings, however, must be interpreted with caution for the reasons mentioned above.

Overall, only 12% of sexual incidents were reported to the police (see Figure 20). More were reported in Scotland (30%), consistent with the higher proportion of assaults. Major reasons for non-reporting were that the incident was "not serious enough" (37%), "solved it myself/perpetrator known" (20%), "inappropriate for police" (8%), "police could do nothing" (9%) and "police won't do anything" (6%).

As would be expected, a much higher proportion of sexual assaults (24%) were reported to the police than incidents of offensive behaviour (6%). Of the cases of rape reported in the survey, 48% were said to have been reported to the police.

Figure 20: Percentage of sexual incidents reported to the police

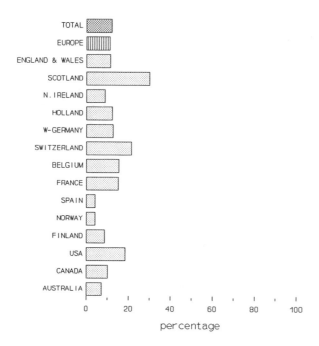

Assaults/threats

The question asked of respondents was:

".... have you been personally attacked or threatened by someone in a way that really frightened you (either at home, or elsewhere, such as in a pub, in the street, at school or at your workplace)."

Risks of assault in 1988 in the USA (5.4%) and Australia (5.2%) approached double the overall average of 2.9% victimized. Risks were also relatively high in Canada (4.0%). In Europe, relatively high rates emerged in the Netherlands (3.4%), W.Germany (3.1%) and Spain (3%). Norway (3%) and Finland (2.9%) emerge higher on the assault ranking than they do for most other crimes, with risks slightly above the European average (Figure 21).

Figure 21: Victimization rates for assaults/threats. Percentage victimized in the past five years and in 1988

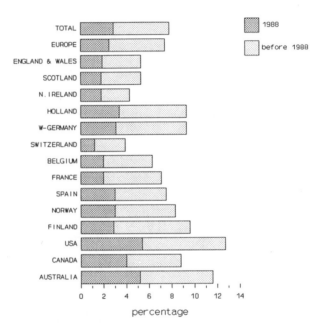

Multiple assault victimization was again rather common: a third of victims reported that they had been assaulted more than once in 1988, and 9% five times or more. Overall, 27% of the victims knew the offender by name, and 12% by sight. In 22% of the assaults by offenders who were known by name to the victim, the offender was a family member. In Canada it was 43% (N=89).

It is notable that both the national victimization rates, as well as the characteristics of assaults, closely correspond with the national findings about sexual incidents. Sexual incidents and assaults/threats seem to be related

36

social phenomena, or reflect similar sensitivities among the public in different countries to incidents of this type.[9]

In 42% of the incidents described, the offender actually used force (as opposed to threatening behaviour). The figure was lower (about a third) in the USA, Spain and Belgium. On the basis of the findings about robbery, this might suggest that in the USA and Spain threats with a weapon were more common. The proportion of incidents which involved force was relatively high in Finland (58%). Of those victims against whom force had been used, overall half had actually suffered injury; a quarter saw a doctor as a result.

Figure 22 presents figures for the number of people who in 1988 experienced assaults with force, and threats in which no force was used.[10] For assaults with force, risks in 1988 were highest in Australia (3.0%) and the USA (2.3%); in Europe, those in Finland (2%), the Netherlands (2%) and W.Germany (1.5%) were most at risk.

Those who experienced assaults with force, were asked whether they were shot, stabbed or otherwise assaulted with a weapon.[11] In 8.5% of the cases, a weapon was used. The percentages were the highest in the Netherlands (15%), France (15%), N.Ireland (14%), the USA (14%) and Canada (12%), although numbers per country were small. Chapter 5 looks at national ownership rates for guns.

---

9. The national victimization rates for threats/assaults and sexual incidents are strongly correlated (Spearman's r=.812). The rank order correlation between assault with force and sexual assault was .534.

10. See footnote 8 for information about the calculation of these rates.

11. In future studies a question about the use of a weapon should also be put to people who experienced threats. There are indications that many of the threats have been quite frightening for the victim (see Chapter 3).

Figure 22: Victimization rates for assaults with force and threats in which no force was used. Percentage victimized in 1988

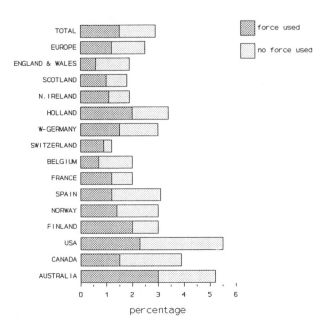

A third of threats and assaults were reported to the police (see Figure 23). Reporting was relatively uncommon in Finland (18%), W.Germany (26%) and Switzerland (26%), though this does not appear to be explained by the fact that the incidents were of a less serious nature. Major reasons for non-reporting were that the incidents were "not serious enough" (36%), "solved it myself" (17%), "inappropriate for the police" (9%), "police could do nothing" (13%), "police won't do anything" (9%), "fear of reprisal" (5%). These reasons were quite similar to those given for not reporting "sexual assaults".

Of the cases of assault with force 37.5% were reported to the police on average. This percentage is still fairly low. In any event, in most countries sexual or violence offences were apparently less readily reported to the police than crimes against property (Table E.4 gives an overview of the reporting rates for different types of crime).

38

Figure 23: Percentage of assaults/threats reported to the police

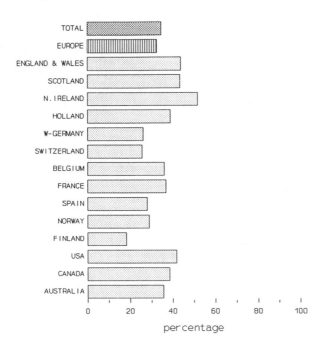

Overall patterns of victimization

It is possible to examine victimization rates for three main categories of crimes.[12] The percentages in Figure 24 (see Table E.5, Annex E for details) refer to respondents who said they had experienced one or more of the *combined* categories of offences in 1988 (thus the figures do not match individual summations). The categories are:

1. *Property crime*: six crimes against property (without violence against persons): theft of cars, motorcycles, and bicycles, theft from a car, car vandalism, and other personal thefts (excluding pickpocketing);
2. *Burglary* (including attempts);

---

12. A factor analysis showed the existence of four separate factors. The same factors were found after varimax (orthogonal) and oblimin (oblique) rotation, which means the four factors are hardly intercorrelated. The first factor was defined by personal thefts, robbery, sexual incidents and threats/assaults, the second factor by theft of motorcycles and bicycles and the third by car theft, theft from a car, and car vandalism. The fourth factor was defined by burglary and attempted burglary. On theoretical grounds we decided to combine the second and third factors, together with personal thefts (excluding pickpocketing), into one category 'property crimes'. The other categories are burglary (the fourth factor) and contact crimes (the first factor, but without non-contact thefts).

3. *Contact crime*: pickpocketing, robbery, sexual incidents, and threats/-assaults.

Figure 24: Victimization rates for property crime, burglary and contact crimes in 1988

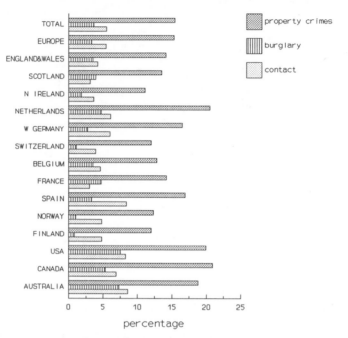

The highest 1988 victimization rates for property crime were found in Canada (20.9%), the Netherlands (20.5%), the USA (19.9%), and Australia (18.8%). The lowest rates were found in N.Ireland (11.1%), Switzerland, Finland (12.0%) and Norway (12.3%).

The highest 1988 victimization rates for burglary were found in the USA (7.5%), Australia (7.3%) and Canada (5.3%). In Europe, risks in the Netherlands and France (4.7%) were highest. Low rates were again found in Switzerland, Norway, Finland and N.Ireland.

For contact crimes (crimes of violence and pickpocketing), the highest were found in Australia (8.6%), the USA (8.3%), Canada (6.9%), and Spain (8.4%). Low rates were found in Scotland, Switzerland, N.Ireland, and France: between 3-4% of respondents had been victimized.

40

Overall victimization percentages for all crimes are given in Figure 25, showing the percentages of people who were victims of any of the crimes covered in the survey in 1988 and over five years.

Figure 25: Overall victimization rates for all crimes. Percentage victim of any crime in 1988 and over five years

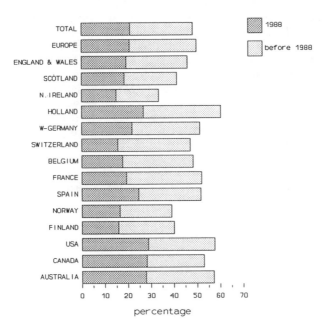

Those most likely to have experienced a crime covered in the survey in 1988 were in the USA (28.8% had done so), Canada (28.1%), and Australia (27.8%). In Europe, those in the Netherlands (26.8%), Spain (24.6%) and W.Germany (21.9%) had higher overall rates than the European average. N.Ireland (15.0%), Switzerland (15.6%), Finland (15.9%) and Norway (16.5) had the lowest overall rates.

The overall prevalence rate for five years is the highest in the Netherlands (60.4%). This percentage is greatly influenced by the extraordinarily high five years prevalence rate for bicycle theft (25%). Other countries with high five years overall prevalence rates are the USA (57.6%), Australia (57.2%), Canada (53%), France (52%), Spain (51.6%), and W.Germany (51.3%).

Incidence victimization rates

As said at the beginning of this chapter, incidence rates are an alternative measure of risk. These express the total number of crimes experienced by the sample as a whole, taking account of people who experienced more than one incident of an offence. Figure 26 shows 1988 incidence risks. The total number of crimes experienced was highest in the USA. Generally speaking, country positions were similar as measured by incidence risks as they were as measured by prevalence risks (r=.934). However, on an incidence measure, Canadians emerge slightly less at risk: that is, although relatively many Canadians experienced a crime counted in the survey, they were less likely to do so on several occasions than those in the USA and Australia. Relatively speaking, risks in England & Wales and Finland were are also slightly lower as indicated by the incidence measure. Conversely, risks in N.Ireland and Belgium were relatively higher on an incidence base than on a prevalence one: although relatively few people were victims in these countries, they were slightly more likely to have experienced more than one crime. Table E.3 in Annex E shows details of incidence rates, by country, for individual offence types.

Figure 26: Overall victimization rates for all crimes in 1988. Number of all crimes counted in the survey, per 100 people

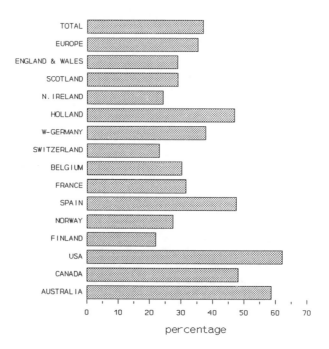

Victimization rates in Warsaw (Poland) and Surabaja (East Java, Indonesia)

Methodological aspects

Surveys using the standardized questionnaire were conducted amongst local populations in Warsaw (Poland) and Surabaja (Indonesia). In Warsaw, fieldwork was done in February 1989 by telephone interviewing (though not with CATI methods). A random sample was drawn from the official telephone register. Interviews were held with 60% of the selected numbers, providing a net sample of 500 respondents. The sample was reweighted according to household size and sex in the same way as the other fourteen countries (but without a special weight for age due to a lack of relevant statistics for Warsaw). In Surabaja (Indonesia), a random stratified sample was drawn through a random walk procedure. It was stratified according to the six districts of the town and reweighted according to sex. The net sample was 600 respondents (100 from each district). The interviews were conducted face-to-face by senior undergraduates in February and March 1989.[13]

Results

Since both Warsaw and Surabaja are large cities where victimization rates are known to be higher, it is inappropriate to compare risks with the national findings from the other fourteen countries. Instead, Polish and Indonesian victimization rates are compared with those of the inhabitants of cities of more than 100,000 inhabitants in (i) the USA, (ii) Canada, (iii) Australia, and (iv) Western Europe. Details are shown in Table 1, which also allows a useful comparison of victimization rates in larger cities. Strictly, a better comparison for Warsaw and Surabaja would have been with towns larger than 1,000,000, though numbers restricted this. Other analysis showed that risks in towns of 500,000 in Europe, Australia and N.America were only slightly higher than those shown below, which are based on towns with 100,000 inhabitants or more.

---

13. The data of both Warsaw and Surabaja have partly been processed at the Research and Documentation Centre of the Ministry of Justice of the Netherlands.

Table 1: Victimization rates for ten types of crime in Warsaw (Poland) and Surabaja (Indonesia) compared to victimization rates in other larger cities (>100,000 inhabitants). Percentage victimized in 1988

	Warsaw Poland	Surabaja Indonesia	USA	Canada	Australia	W.Europe
Theft of car	2.2	0.2	3.6	1.0	2.4	1.6
Theft from car	10.2	4.7	12.2	8.9	8.1	8.4
Car vandalism	7.6	2.7	13.0	12.2	9.4	8.0
Motorcycle theft	0.0	0.8	0.3	0.5	0.4	0.3
Bicycle theft	1.0	2.7	3.1	3.6	1.4	2.6
Owners						
Theft of car	3.5	0.4	3.8	1.1	2.7	2.3
Theft from car	16.5	10.8	13.0	10.4	9.2	11.8
Car vandalism	12.3	6.2	13.9	14.3	10.7	11.3
Motorcycle theft	0.0	1.0	2.9	6.5	5.7	3.3
Bicycle theft	2.2	4.1	4.5	5.4	3.1	5.5
Burglary/entry	2.6	3.8	4.1	3.9	4.7	2.9
Attempted burglary	2.8	1.7	8.4	4.1	5.6	2.3
Robbery	1.2	0.5	2.6	1.8	0.9	2.0
Personal thefts	13.4	5.2	5.9	6.5	4.7	5.8
Pickpocketing	13.0	3.3	1.5	1.8	0.9	3.3
Sexual incidents[1]	1.8	3.2	4.1	2.3	4.0	1.5
Sexual assaults	1.0	0.8	1.5	0.7	1.3	0.5
Assaults/threats	3.0	0.8	6.6	4.0	6.3	3.3
Assaults with force	1.4	0.3	2.0	1.6	4.0	1.1
All crimes	34.4	20.0	38.3	32.9	30.8	26.4
N Total respondents	500	600	392	942	700	5484
N Car owners	310	260	368	804	619	3907
N Motorcycle owners	21	515	35	77	53	486
N Bicycle owners	228	389	266	633	326	2553

1) Percentage based on all respondents, not women only

Table 1 shows, first, that victimization rates in larger cities in the USA are generally higher than elsewhere. Exceptions were that general and owner's risks of bicycle and motorcycle thefts were higher in Canada and risks of burglary with entry in Australia. Also thefts of personal property were much higher in Warsaw.

Victimization rates in large urban areas in Canada and W.Europe are not greatly dissimilar, though Canadian vehicle owners were rather more at risk of car vandalism and motorcycle theft, and Canadians generally slightly more of burglary with entry and sexual incidents; in Europe pickpocketing was commoner.

In Australian cities, risks are below those in Europe for some crimes (eg, theft from cars, bicycle theft and robbery), but above them for others (eg, burglary of both kinds, sexual assault and assaults with force). Risks in Australian cities are generally below those in the USA and Canada, particularly the USA. As said, though, burglary risks in Australia were highest.

Victimization rates in Warsaw (Poland) are not very dissimilar from those in the larger other European cities, although thefts for car owners are somewhat higher and thefts of personal property, in particular pickpocketing, are much more common.

Victimization rates in Surabaja (Indonesia) show a somewhat different picture. Motorcycle theft, though far from a common offence, is relatively more common in Surabaja, where there is an extraordinarily high ownership rate (86%). The owner's risk is relatively low. Car-related crimes are relatively low in Surabaja though ownership is low (43% of households own a car). The burglary rate in Surabaja is relatively high. Offensive sexual behaviour was quite frequently reported too, though cultural and definitional differences may well play a part here. The percentage of respondents who report assaults/threats is extremely low.

Since attitudes towards the police, victim assistance etc. are less strongly related to level of urbanization, findings about these are presented jointly with those of the other fourteen countries in the next chapters.

A preliminary analysis of international differences

It will be for future analysis to explore in depth how victimization rates are related to global cultural, social and economic characteristics of the countries in the survey, and to the differential opportunities and conditions they offer for crimes of different types. For the moment, results from some preliminary analyses are presented.

General findings

There was no association between overall national victimization rates and Gross National Product per capita. There was a positive relationship, though, between GNP and the mean value of the stolen property per country (r=.497). There was also a positive relationship between national ownership rates of cars and overall victimization rates (r=.543).[14] This suggests that neither poverty nor wealth is associated with higher crime in any simple sense, but that wealth may affect opportunities for property crime. More complex analysis will be appropriate to examine this fully, though some findings on the relationship between vehicle ownership and vehicle crime specifically are presented later.

As has been mentioned earlier, the distribution of housing types was not clearly related to national victimization rates either, although the high

---

14. The rank order correlation between rates of national ownership of cars and the five year prevalence rates is .543. The correlation between ownership and the 1988 prevalence rate is .508.

burglary rate in Australia may be related to its large number of semi- and detached houses.

Finally, no association was found between the national rates of going out in the evening and national victimization rates for all crimes (and for contact crimes in particular).[15]

Urbanization

National victimization rates are positively correlated with levels of urbanization, as would be expected from previous research (r=.640). Countries with fewer persons living in cities of 100,000 or more tend to have lower overall victimization rates, and *vice versa* (Figure 27). (Further details of the figures are given in Table E.6, Annex E.)

Canada (45%), Spain (45%) and Australia (35%) have higher than average numbers of residents in cities of 100,000 or more; low percentages are found in N.Ireland, Belgium, Switzerland and Norway. In the USA and the Netherlands (where about 20% live in cities) victimization rates are high relative to the number living in cities.

---

15. Chapter 3 presents data about the relationship between the frequency of outdoor visits in the evening for recreational purposes and victimization rates at the level of individual respondents. For all crime categories, those who went out most were more at risk.

Figure 27: Overall national victimization rates and national rates of city dwellers, of 14 countries

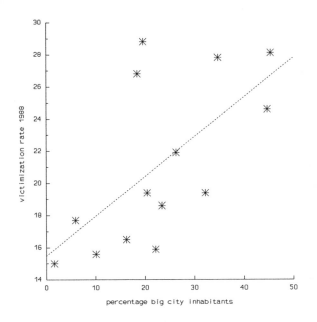

Vehicle ownership

For offences involving vehicles - cars, motorcycles (including moped and scooters), and bicycles - there is good reason to consider victimization risks for owners only: *owner prevalence rates*. Levels of ownership vary considerably across countries. For instance, 91% of all Dutch households possessed at least one bicycle, compared to 31% of Scottish families; 95% of the sample in the USA owned cars, as against less than 70% in Spain and Scotland. Furthermore, there are also differences in how many vehicles these households have. (For instance, the mean number of bicycles per household in the Netherlands was 2.5, as against 1.3 for the total sample; the mean number of cars per household in the USA was 2.2 as against 1.2 for all countries). Thus, it is of some interest also to consider risks for *vehicles* themselves: *vehicle incidence rates*. Table E.7 in Annex E shows 1988 vehicle incidence rates.

Risks of vehicle offences will of course be higher on the basis of owners only than on the basis of the whole population. Table 2 shows 1988 prevalence rates for owners of thefts of cars, thefts from cars, car vandalism, motorcycle theft and bicycle theft. (Table E.8 in Annex E shows 5-year risks

47

for vehicle crime, based on owners.) Differences between national prevalence rates for owners tend to be somewhat smaller than between population prevalence rates, though in general the relative vulnerability of owners in different countries is broadly similar to the picture presented earlier on a population base.

Table 2: Victimization rates for vehicle crimes. Percentage of owners victimized in 1988

	Theft of cars	Theft from cars	Car vandalism	Motorcycle theft	Bicycle theft
Total	1.4	6.6	8.4	3.1	4.4
Europe	1.6	7.4	9.0	3.0	3.9
England & Wales	2.4	7.3	8.8	0.8	2.8
Scotland	1.2	7.7	9.4	7.1	3.2
N.Ireland	2.2	5.5	6.1	3.7	3.5
Netherlands	0.4	6.8	10.6	3.2	8.3
W.Germany	0.5	5.8	10.8	1.8	4.4
Switzerland	0.0	2.4	5.2	4.8	4.6
Belgium	1.0	3.3	8.0	2.9	4.6
France	2.8	7.1	7.6	3.6	2.5
Spain	1.9	14.6	9.2	3.9	2.6
Norway	1.4	3.5	5.7	3.1	3.8
Finland	0.5	3.5	5.2	0.0	3.5
USA	2.2	9.7	9.3	1.0	4.6
Canada	0.9	8.1	11.0	3.4	5.4
Australia	2.6	7.8	9.9	2.6	4.0

Amongst owners, the risks of having a car stolen in 1988 were highest in France (2.8%), Australia (2.6%), England & Wales (2.4%), N.Ireland (2.2%) and the USA (2.2%) - a similar picture as from population-based rates. Five-year rates for owners were similarly distributed, though on this measure owners in Scotland were rather more at risk. When risks per target are examined (vehicle incidence rates), cars in Spain and N.Ireland are most likely to be stolen. Risks for vehicles in France, England & Wales, and Australia are still high.

For thefts from cars, risks among car-owners in 1988 were by far the highest in Spain (14.6% of owners were victimized). Relatively high rates were also found in the three non-European countries, and risks in Scotland, England & Wales, and France were higher than in other parts of Europe. This picture is similar to that from population-based rates. Five-year rates for owners also show a generally similar picture, though risks in Switzerland and France were slightly lower relatively speaking. Vehicle incidence rates show cars in Spain to be at higher risk of thefts than any elsewhere. Cars in Scotland were also quite vulnerable.

For car vandalism, prevalence rates for owners in 1988 were highest in Canada (11.0%), W.Germany (10.8%), and the Netherlands (10.6%). In Scotland and Spain, where there were relatively few car owners, car vandalism risks were higher than indicated on a population base: the relatively few owners in these countries were at relatively high risk. In the USA, in contrast, the fact that most of the population owned cars means that owners in the USA are rather less at risk relatively speaking than appears from a population measure. The picture from five-year risks amongst owners were generally similar, though owners in Canada were relatively a little less vulnerable on five-year figures, and those in France rather more. Looking at targets, cars in the Netherlands, Spain, W.Germany, and Scotland were most frequently vandalised. In Canada, cars were less at risk relatively than other measures of risk suggest.

For motorcycle owners, those in Scotland (7.1%) were at far the highest risk in 1988, though not as noticeably so over the last five years. Risks in Scotland were higher relatively measured on an owner-base than on a population base; the same was true in N.Ireland. Risks among owners in 1988 were also high in Switzerland (4.8%). Considering both 1988 and 5 year measures, relatively high risks also emerged in France and Spain. Vehicle incidence rates show highest risks for motorcycles in Scotland and Switzerland.

In the Netherlands, 8.3% of owners reported a bicycle theft in 1988. Risks were also relatively high in Canada (5.4%), Switzerland, Belgium the USA (all 4.6%). This picture is similar to that on a population base, though risks in Belgium were rather higher, relatively, amongst owners. Incidence rates for bicycles themselves show a similar picture.

Opportunity and vehicle theft

The relationship between national vehicle ownership rates and national victimization risks merits some discussion. In general, countries with higher rates of ownership of vehicles of different kinds had higher levels of offences involving these vehicles.[16] Figures 28 and 29 show the particularly close relationship between ownership levels and bicycle theft and motorcycle theft respectively.

These results mean that the estimated numbers of cars, motorcycles and bicycles stolen per 100 population are higher in countries with more cars, etc. per 100 population. The results from Warsaw and Surabaja confirm the existence of this relationship.

---

16. The rank order correlation between risks of thefts of cars and ownership of cars was r=.363; for thefts from cars, r=.226; car vandalism, r=.648. For motorcycle thefts and ownership of motorcycles the correlation was r=.741. For bicycle ownership and bike theft, r=.890. For theft offences involving cars, Spanish results are out of line, with low ownership, but rather high risks.

Figure 28: Victimization rate for bicycle theft and national rates of ownership of bicycles, 14 countries

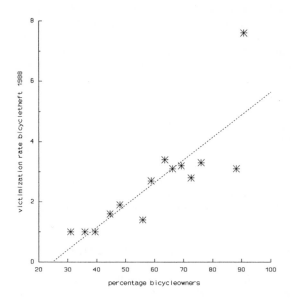

Ownership levels of bicycles are the highest in the Netherlands (91%) and Finland (88%). In the Netherlands the rate for bicycle theft is extremely high. In Finland it is somewhat lower than was to be expected on the basis of the level of ownership. The other countries are closely in line with the correlation.

Figure 29: Victimization rates for motorcycle thefts and national rates of ownership of motorcycles, 14 countries

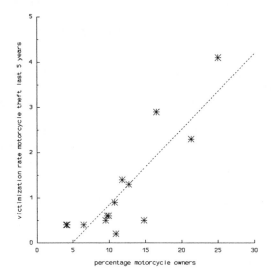

The levels of ownership of motorcycles are the highest in Switzerland, Spain and France. Victimization rates for motorcycle theft are clearly the highest in these countries as well.

It might be argued that the association between ownership and risk simply reflects the fact that since non-owners cannot by definition be subject to vehicle crime, overall victimization rates are bound to be lower in countries with low ownership rates. This argument, however, does not explain the fact that where targets are relatively plentiful, risks among owners do not decrease. Rather, owners have higher risks in countries with higher ownership levels, measured by both the proportion of households owning vehicles, and the number of vehicles per 100 population.[17]

Broadly, these results suggest that a plentiful supply of vehicles itself generates more crime. They go against the notion that vehicle crime levels are dictated by the activities of a 'fixed' supply of offenders, who will prey upon targets when they are in short supply, thus making risks among

---

17. A measure of target availability is the number of vehicles per 100 population. Comparing prevalence risks for owners against this shows that risks increase as availability does. The product moment correlations were r=.361 for theft of cars, .205 for thefts from cars, .303 for car vandalism, .031 for motorcycle theft; and .745 for bicycle theft. Similar correlations are found when risks for owners are compared to the proportion of households owning vehicles. In both cases, the association between availability and risk is strongest for bicycle theft. Spearman's rank order correlations showed similar coefficients.

owners higher where there are fewer vehicles for offender to steal, or steal from. Instead, offenders seem to be more criminally active when they have an ample supply of targets. This may be because there is a better choice of vehicles to pick from for joyriding, dealing for profit, or stealing of stereos and radios. There may also be a larger pool of people who want to use such vehicles but cannot legally do so.

Bicycle theft appears to be particularly driven by availability. Not only do risks for owners increase in line with ownership levels, but so too does the risk for individual bicycles themselves.[18] This is evidenced particularly by the Netherlands where alongside the highest ownership level go highest risks for owners of bikes and highest risks for individual bicycles. One might speculate that where bicycles are very plentiful, this itself sets up a process of opportunist thieving, which is made easy simply by virtue of the many bicycles around to steal. It may also promote a healthy fencing structure. Research in the Netherlands has also found that some multiple victims of bicycle theft compensate their losses by stealing bikes themselves (Van Dijk, 1986).

Bicycle theft and car theft

Bicycle theft risks were *negatively* related to risks of car theft: risks of car thefts, in other words, are lower in countries where bicycles are more common (see Figure 30). The Spearman's rank order correlation was -.789. This is not explained by the fact that in countries where bicycles were most common there were fewer cars (bicycle and car ownership are actually positively related). Vehicles will be stolen for various reasons (eg, financial gain, joyriding and a means of temporary transportation) - though it is difficult to substantiate empirically the contribution of each (cf. Mayhew et al., 1989). Where transport is the purpose of theft and there are plenty of bicycles around, these findings suggest that many offenders will make do with a bicycle. On the market of illegal transportation, bicycles could be a substitute for cars, if bicycles are in sufficient supply.

---

18. The product moment correlation between the number of bicycles per 100 population and the number of thefts per 100 bicycles was .410. (The rank order correlation was positive, but lower (.143), with Scotland and Finland out of line.) For other offences, the relationship between the two measures was even weaker but still positive. For theft from cars, and car vandalism, a negative relationship appears (though not statistically significantly so). As the number of cars per 100 population increases, risks per vehicle decrease. It might be for these two offences that a type of 'saturation effect' operates. In countries with relatively many cars per 100 population further increases in the number of cars may not lead to a *proportional* increase in the number of crimes committed. In some countries, the number of cars may have reached a level where further increases do not lead to more crime at all. Clearly, the relationships between opportunity and vehicle-related crime deserve further study.

Consistent with this is that lower car theft rates were found in countries where bicycles outnumber cars (r=.702). For example, the lowest car theft rates are found in Switzerland, the Netherlands, Finland and W.Germany: in each of these countries there were three or more bicycles owned for each car.

Also consistent with the notion that opportunistic vehicle thieves will suffice with a bicycle if there are enough of them, would be that in countries where there are few bicycles to draw upon, more cars will be stolen, used temporarily and then left to be found by the police or owners. The data bear this out. High rates of recovery of stolen cars were found in England & Wales (77%), France (76%), Scotland (78%) and Australia (84%) - where car theft is commonest and bicycle ownership low. Lower rates of recovery were found in W.Germany (56%), Switzerland (51%), Belgium (61%), and the Netherlands (67%).

Figure 30: Victimization rate for car theft and victimization rate for bicycle theft, 14 countries

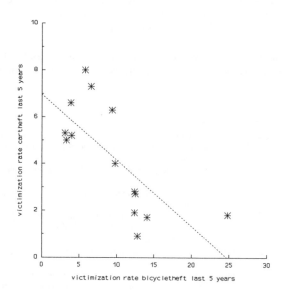

Victimization rates and police recorded crime

Are the survey results at all in line with figures of offences recorded by the police, as compiled for different countries by Interpol? Because of how police offence categories are defined, only certain offences can be matched:

theft of vehicles, burglary, robbery, assault, and sexual offences.[19] The main comparisons are between average figures from Interpol returns for 1982-86 (to iron out year to year fluctuations), and 5-year prevalence victimization rates from the survey. (Table E.9 and Table E.10 in Annex E shows details of the figures.) The findings can only be suggestive. A number of technical issues undermine the comparability of the figures.[20] More important, it is unlikely that police figures themselves compare 'like with like' exactly. Recorded offences are highly susceptible to differences in police recording practices, and to inconsistencies as regards the offence categories into which different types of incidents are put.

Two main comparisons can be made. The first is between recorded offences and estimates from the survey of the amount of crime experienced, whether or not reported to the police. The second uses survey estimates of the number of crimes which are reported to the police.[21] This is an important adjustment since the number of offences which the police can potentially record will largely depend on how many are reported to them by victims. Survey results have also shown that, for robbery and theft of cars, people in a few countries were much more likely than others to have been victimized abroad. It is also useful, then, to take account of this by considering only offences which took place within the victim's own country.

All the comparisons below focus on how far the survey and police measures show similar *relative rankings* of countries with regard to crime levels. The

---

19. Specifically, the comparisons where for:
    Theft of vehicles: Survey: excluding motorbikes and bicycles
    Interpol: commercial and private vehicles (often undefined). (Switzerland excluded). Category 4.2.
    Burglary: Survey: (i) completed residential burglaries; (ii) completed and attempted burglaries
    Interpol: all burglary (residential and commercial). Category 4.1.2.
    Robbery: Survey: as defined.
    Interpol: robbery and violent theft (excluding burglary). Category 4.1.1
    Assaults: Survey: (i) assaults/threats; (ii) assaults with force
    Interpol: serious assault. Category 3
    Sexual offences: Survey: (i) sexual incidents against women; (ii) sexual assaults against women
    Interpol: Sexual offences. USA excluded. Category 2.
    Annual returns are not always made to Interpol. Additional crime figures were collected from other sources where possible.
20. For one, there is sampling error on the survey figures. Second, in the comparisons made, police rates are incidence ones (crimes per 100,000 population), whereas the only survey measure for the 5-year period is a prevalence one. Third, police statistics cover crimes against the total population, while survey rates are based on people aged 16 or more; this may affect comparisons of sexual offences and assaults most. Fourth, police statistics count crime within the country, whether against residents or not; the survey counts crime against residents whether they were victimized inside the country or not. Potentially, this might affect the comparisons of robbery and vehicle crime most, though some account is taken of this. Finally, only a crude calculation could be made of 5-year survey figures for assaults with force, and for sexual assaults, using estimates from the 1988 percentages.
21. Reporting figures for the 'last incident' which occurred over the 5-year period are taken.

amount of crime that each measure shows will of course be different. (Table E.11 in Annex E shows details of the rank order correlations between survey figures and offences recorded by the police for the various comparisons made.)

The strongest correspondence between the survey measure and offences recorded by the police is for car thefts (see Figure 31). The rank order correlation was .786, and even higher when survey figures were adjusted for 'own country' offences (.813). The main discrepancies between survey and police figures are that Norway has a lower relative risk according to the survey (2.7%) than according to recorded offences (463); conversely, Belgium has a slightly higher one (4.0%) than is to be expected on the basis of police figures (150).

Adjusting survey victimization rates by levels of reporting to the police made little difference to the association between survey estimates and police figures for theft of cars. This is not surprising given that the vast majority of car thefts are reported in all countries.

Figure 31: Victimization rate for car theft in the last five years versus car thefts per 100,000 inhabitants, 1982-1986, as recorded by the police, 14 countries

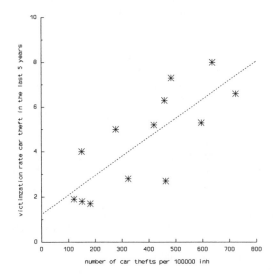

There is a moderately strong positive correlation between the two sources of information for burglary, both using a survey measure of burglaries with entry (.442), and one which included attempted burglaries. In France, relative risks are higher according to police records than according to the survey, while in the Netherlands and W.Germany the reverse is true. Taking the level of *reported* burglaries with entry only, there was a very slight improvement in the relationship between the survey measure and police figures (.473).[22]

The relationship between survey and police figures for robbery is not particularly strong (.371), though becomes more so when offences committed abroad are omitted (.618), and reported offences only are considered (.666). With the survey measures of reported crime, the principal discrepancies are that N.Ireland and Scotland have comparatively high levels of robbery according to police figures, whereas the survey indicates low rankings; in contrast, robbery risks in W.Germany and Belgium are relatively lower according to police figures than according to the survey.

The survey measure of assaults/threats shows little correspondence with the picture from recorded offences (.037). (There is even a negative relationship when only assaults with force are considered, though this may well be due to measurement error.) In particular, recorded crime shows England & Wales and N.Ireland as having relatively high risks, though survey positions are lower. The reporting rate for assaults in these two countries was relatively high (47% and 50% respectively; the average rate being 31%). In contrast, risks for assault/threats in Finland and Australia are higher relatively speaking on survey figures. In Finland the reporting rate was indeed relatively low (10%). This was not the case in Australia, though (see table E.4). On the basis of reported offences, however, there was a much closer relationship between survey and police figures (.653).

Survey and police figures do not seem to give a particularly similar picture for sexual assaults (which are small in number and therefore unstable), or sexual incidents (.247). This is mainly because two countries in particular are out of line. Relatively high risks are registered in Spain in the survey, but very low ones in police records; conversely, there are relatively low risks from the survey for Scotland, but high ones according to police figures. Again, however, on the basis of reported offences, the relationship between the two measures becomes much closer (.835). This is partly accounted for by the relatively low reporting rate in Spain (4%) and the relatively high reporting rate in Scotland (30%).

In sum, then, the picture of relative levels of victimization as indicated by the survey is not very closely in accord with that from recorded crime figures, except for theft of vehicles. For other offences, rankings for burglary and robbery are closest. These findings parallel those from work in the USA which looked at city measures of crime according to police figures and results from the US National Crime Survey (Cohen and Lichbach, 1982; Cohen and Land, 1984): this also showed the closest correspondence for

---

22. Reporting to the police was not asked about for attempted burglary. As the reporting of attempts (which will be included in offences recorded by the police) may differ across country, the comparison here should be regarded cautiously.

vehicle theft, and the weakest for assault; measures of burglary and robbery showed modest associations at city level.

The present results show that the dissimilarity in country rankings is partly due to a few countries being out of line on the survey or police measures. However, the most important result of the analysis was that there is a much closer correspondence in relative risks of crime when account is taken of differences in reporting to the police. After adjusting for national reporting rates, the associations between survey measures and police figures were statistically robust for all five crime types. This result adds to the credibility of the survey methods employed. It also confirms the belief that levels of recorded offences are likely to be unstable for comparative purposes *simply* on account of how often the police are told about crime by victims in various jurisdictions. Even taking reporting into consideration, however, still leaves many discrepancies in the picture of relative risks in different countries. Measurement error on survey figures will play a part here, but so too will differences in how the police in different countries record particular offences.

3 Offences and victims

Place of crime

Information was gathered for seven types of crime about the place where the crime had been committed. In order to see whether there are consistent national differences in this respect, data for all types of crime are combined.

Table 3 shows that 4% of all victimizations were committed outside the victim's own country. The proportion of victimizations abroad was somewhat higher in Switzerland (16%), Finland (9%), W.Germany (8%), and Belgium (8%).

Chapter 2 showed that for these four countries, thefts from cars were relatively common abroad, as was theft of cars for W.Germans and Belgians. Robbery was common abroad for the first three countries, while thefts of personal property (perhaps notably pickpocketing) was a relatively common experience, too, for Swiss and Finns away from home.

In the Netherlands, relatively many victims were victimized outside their own home town area. In Australia, relatively many were victimized in their own area, but not near their home. This was in particular the case with car vandalism.

Table 3: Distribution of crimes over various places in %

	Near home	Elsewhere in local area	Elsewhere in country	Abroad	Don't know	Total sample
Total	45	37	12	4	1	100
Europe	47	35	12	4	1	100
England & Wales	46	41	10	3	1	100
Scotland	54	35	7	2	1	100
N.Ireland	47	38	12	3	<1	100
Netherlands	39	33	21	5	2	100
W.Germany	46	35	10	8	1	100
Switzerland	32	34	18	16	<1	100
Belgium	37	34	18	8	3	100
France	49	35	14	2	1	100
Spain	55	32	11	<1	2	100
Norway	48	37	7	4	3	100
Finland	48	31	10	9	2	100
USA	47	40	12	1	<1	100
Canada	48	42	8	2	<1	100
Australia	39	50	8	2	2	100

Victim characteristics

The distribution of victimization risks for the various crimes covered in the survey allows much in-depth analysis. Attention is paid here mainly to 1988 risks in terms of gender, age, size of place of residence (townsize), level of income (Table 4), and frequency of going out for social reasons in the evening (Table 5).

Table 4: Victimization rates for three categories of crime (1) and all crime, by different groups of the population

	Property crime	Burglary	Contact crime	Any crime	Total respondents
	% victimized once or more				
Gender					
Male	16.7	3.7	5.1	22.0	13,542
Female	14.2	3.6	6.0	20.3	14,458
Total	15.4	3.6	5.5	21.1	28,000
Age					
16-34	21.1	4.5	8.9	28.9	10,716
35-54	16.7	3.9	4.3	22.0	9,048
55+	6.5	2.3	2.5	10.1	8,138
Household income (2)					
Below average	11.7	3.5	5.4	17.6	12,046
Above average	19.8	3.9	5.9	25.6	11,794
Not stated	13.5	3.2	4.8	18.6	4,121
Size of place of residence					
<10,000	12.5	2.5	4.0	16.7	9,317
10,000-50,000	15.1	3.3	5.3	20.8	6,408
>50,000	19.7	5.2	7.7	27.5	8,490
Not stated	13.3	3.6	5.1	18.5	3,785

Notes:
1. *Property crime*: theft of cars, motorcycles, bicycles; theft from cars; car vandalism; non-contact personal thefts.
   Burglary: including attempts.
   Contact crime: pickpocketing; robbery; sexual incidents; assaults/threats.
2. Respondents were asked first whether or not their total household income after deductions was above or below a given figures (set in the questionnaire at the median level for the country). They were then asked whether it was above or below the upper or lower quartile figure (as appropriate). Quartile figures were set independently in each country on the basis of national income data.

Victimization rates for property crimes (vehicle thefts and non-contact personal thefts) were higher for men, people between 16 to 35 years, households with an above average income, and inhabitants of larger cities. These differences are partly but not wholly caused by higher ownerships rates of cars. Age seems to be the most important differentiating factor; people above 55 have substantially lower victimization risks.

Victimization rates for burglary (including attempts) show smaller differences between the various population groups. People younger than 35, and inhabitants of larger cities, faced highest risks of having their home burgled.

Higher victimization rates for contact crimes were also found among younger people, and inhabitants of larger cities. The notion that older people are more vulnerable to robbery, for instance, is refuted by the findings. The victimization rate for robbery is 0.6% for those aged 35 or older, and 1.5% for those younger than this.

Gender differences

Victimization risks for contact crimes were higher for females than for males, though this is in part explained by the fact that questions on sexual assaults were only put to women. Women are also likely to face higher risks of pickpocketing, presumably because more of them carry their purses in a bag than males. Thefts of personal property in which there was no contact with the offender was only a little higher among men (2.8%) than among women (2.5%). Nearly twice as many men (1.2%) reported a robbery in 1988 than women (0.7%). Men were also at more risk of assaults/threats (3.3%) than women (2.5%).

For all offences where the respondents talked about their household's experience (vehicle offences, and burglary), it might be expected that no substantial differences in risks according to gender should be apparent: ie, whoever was interviewed might be thought equally likely to remember and report what had happened in their household. In the event, however, this was not quite the case in all countries (though sampling error may explain some of the gender differences). In general, however, male respondents reported more offences involving cars (theft of and from cars, and car vandalism). One explanation for this is that in single-adult households men more often have cars than women. For burglary with entry, risks were slightly higher for men in general. Risks for attempted burglary were not significantly related to gender.

Going out

Table 5 presents the relationship between victimization and lifestyle, measured by the frequency of outdoor visits in the evening for recreational purposes. For all crime categories, those who went out most were more at risk. This could be because they were more exposed to crimes committed in public areas such as pubs and public transport, as well as to burglaries of their (unattended) houses.

Table 5: Frequency of outdoor evening activities and 1988 victimization rates

	Almost daily	At least once week	At least once a month	Less	Never	Don't know
	% victimized					
Theft of car	1.8	1.3	1.2	0.7	0.7	0.6
Theft from car	7.9	6.4	4.8	3.9	2.6	3.4
Car vandalism	10.4	7.7	6.3	5.5	2.9	4.1
Theft of motorcycle	0.6	0.4	0.4	0.4	0.1	0.3
Theft of bicycle	3.7	3.2	2.3	2.3	0.9	1.4
Burglary with entry	2.8	2.2	1.9	1.6	1.8	1.9
Attempted burglary	2.8	2.2	2.1	1.7	1.2	1.3
Robbery	1.7	1.0	0.7	0.6	0.9	0.3
Personal theft	7.7	4.8	3.0	2.4	2.4	2.0
Sexual incidents	2.6	1.6	1.0	0.8	0.2	0.6
Assaults/threats	6.7	3.4	2.1	1.9	1.3	0.8
Total	50.5	36.0	26.7	23.3	16.4	18.7

Independent risk factors

Preliminary multivariate analyses were undertaken to see which factors in the 14 main participating countries were most important in explaining the overall level of victimization risk.[1] Such analyses take into account any interrelationship between the explanatory variables and show which is most important independent of any other.

The most important risk factor, independent of others, was age. Those under 30 were most at risk and those of 60 and over the least. The second factor was townsize: those in towns or cities of 500,000 or more inhabitants were most vulnerable and those in towns with less than 50,000 the least. The third most important factor was above average household income, which is taken up below. Fourth in determining vulnerability to crime was the extent of evening activities: those who went out at least once a week were most at risk.

In this analysis, gender was not independently related to victimization risk, though this could well be because women were potentially vulnerable to a higher count of crime as only they were asked about sexual incidents.

---

1. The data were analyzed with the techniques of regression, Homals and loglinear analysis. Each of these yielded roughly the same picture. In some runs the variable of income was replaced by level of education, with a similar result (high levels of education being a risk factor of some importance, just as income). If both income and education were included, income proved to be the most relevant risk factor.

High income as a risk factor

As said, the third most important factor relating to both overall victimization risks, and to most offence categories looked at individually, was household income (see note 2, Table 4 for measurement of income).[2] Even controlling for vehicle ownership, risks were highest among those with incomes in the third and fourth quartile - ie, with incomes above average. It can be seen from Figure 32 that the picture is one in which there is a linear progression of risk with income.

Figure 32: Victimization rates for all crimes for four different income groups (quartiles), 14 countries

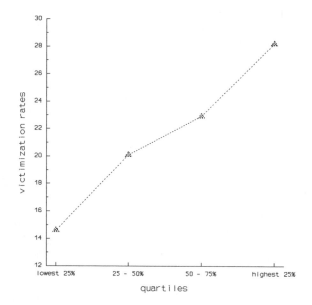

The results on income are of particular interest. For one, they bear on the question (taken up in Chapter 6) of the potential bias from the survey having been carried out solely among more affluent households with telephones. For another, they suggest that the more affluent are frequent

---

2. Taking all 14 main countries together, risks were *higher* for those with above average household income for: car crimes, (controlling for ownership), bicycle theft, and non-contact personal thefts. The higher-income group reported lower risks of sexual incidents. Risks were generally similar across income groups for burglary, robbery, pickpocketing and assaults/threats.

targets of crime because they own more property attractive to offenders (or carry more of it on them).

For all property crimes, the estimated mean values of the stolen property were much higher for the above average income groups (in most countries twice as high). These higher costs per crime will be partly offset, however, by a higher degree of a insurance among the higher income groups.

Within country results

Were gender, age, etc equally important in explaining the pattern of risks at the level of individual countries? In all countries, the linear relationship held between the frequency of going out in the evening and risks of overall victimization: those going out more were more often victimized. For example, those who go out for recreational purposes at least once a week, had risks above 40 percent in the USA, Australia and France. Those who go out less than once a month had risks below 10 percent in France. Their risks were 19% in the USA and 11% in Australia.

For other variables, the overall pattern remained strong, though there were minor deviations. In looking at these results, age, size of place of residence and income are considered below first, after which a word is said about the results of Warsaw and Surabaja and about differences in risk by race in the USA. Risks between men and women in different countries are then taken up in a little more detail in the following section.

Those aged 16-24 years were most at risk in all countries, while risks consistently decreased with age; those older than 65 were in all countries the least vulnerable group. In seven countries, there was a perfect linear relationship between age and victimization (risks decreased with age); this was true in Scotland, the Netherlands, W.Germany, the USA, Canada, Australia, and Spain. Elsewhere, there were only minor deviations from this pattern.

In all countries the risks of those aged 16-24 year were at least three times higher than of those older than 65. Of the young in the USA 51.4% had been victimized in 1988 and only 11% of the elderly. Of the elderly in Norway, Finland, Switzerland and N.Ireland less than 6% had been a victim.

In eleven of the fourteen countries, risks were positively related to townsize. In Australia, those living in towns of less than 50,000 inhabitants had lower risks, as elsewhere, although risks did not differ in larger cities. In France and Switzerland, townsize was not as consistently related to overall risks, though the number of respondents living in larger cities of various sizes was small. (Over half those in France and Switzerland lived in towns of less than 10,000 inhabitants.) Townsize was also less consistently related to overall victimization risk in England & Wales.

The highest victimization risks were found in the cities with more than 500,000 inhabitants in the USA (38.7%) and the Netherlands (37.2%). The lowest in small towns in Scotland (15.2%), Norway (14.8%), Finland (13.5%), and N.Ireland (15.3%), and in Switzerland generally. The safest towns with more than 100,000 inhabitants were in Switzerland.

In nearly all countries, risks were highest among those with the highest incomes and lowest among those with the lowest incomes. The only exception to this was the Netherlands, with highest risks for those with the lowest income. In the Netherlands, the risks for those with incomes below the average are increased by the high rate of bicycle theft. When these thefts are excluded, the general pattern of highest risks for the upper quartiles emerges here also.

Risks below ten percent are found among those with the lowest incomes in England & Wales, Belgium, Finland, Switzerland and N.Ireland. Risks above thirty percent are found among the highest income groups in the USA, Canada, Australia, the Netherlands and Spain, as well as among the lowest income group in the Netherlands. The differences in risks according to income level are larger in countries with lower average risks.

In Poland (Warsaw) overall risks were unrelated to income and weakly related to age. Risks were moderately strong related to the frequency of going out in the evening.

In Indonesia (East Java/Surabaja) risks were unrelated to age and frequency of going out. Those with relatively high incomes (above 150 ECU's per month) had much higher risks. Ethnicity (Indonesian-Chinese) was not related to risk.

In the USA, a question was asked about ethnic background.[3] Respondents who said they were black, Hispanic or Asian had higher victimization risks than others (in the case of burglary and contact crime twice as high). These differences persisted after controlling for vehicle ownership. They may reflect the fact that a higher concentration of non-whites live in riskier areas.

Gender, victimization risks and employment

As mentioned earlier, men face slightly higher risks for vehicle related crimes. Exceptions to this were that a statistically significantly greater

---

3. Non-whites comprised 15.6% of the US sample as against 14.6% of those aged 16 or more in USA generally (US Department of Commerce, 1989).

number of thefts from cars were reported by women in Scotland, and more bicycle thefts by women in the USA.[4]

For burglary with entry, men tended to report slightly more offences than women. In Canada, USA, Belgium and Spain this was not the case - although the higher risks among women were not statistically significant. For attempted burglary, there was generally little difference in risks according to gender that could not be put down to sampling error.

As mentioned earlier, the results confirmed - as do most other independent surveys - that men are more at risk of violent offences. Thus, men were more vulnerable to robbery, and this was so particularly in Canada, Australia and Spain; women in the USA appeared no less at risk than men. While in all countries, men were also at greater risk of assaults/threats, the difference was particularly noticeable in N.Ireland, France, England & Wales, the Netherlands, Spain and W.Germany. For assaults with force, the difference was generally even more pronounced. Men in N.Ireland and France in particular were substantially more at risk than women, though there was relatively less difference in risks for assaults with force between men and women in the USA, Finland, Switzerland, Belgium and Scotland.

For non-contact thefts of personal property, there was, as said earlier, generally little difference between risks for men and women. However, statistically significantly more men than women reported such thefts in Switzerland and N.Ireland. Pickpocketing - generally more of a problem for women - was significantly so for women in N.Ireland, the Netherlands, W.Germany, France and Spain.

Looking at overall victimization, risks were higher for men in all countries, except the USA, Australia, and Scotland. Risks were higher for women in the USA and Scotland even if sexual incidents were excluded. Gender differences were also relatively narrow in England & Wales, Norway, and Canada. They appeared largest in Switzerland, Finland, the Netherlands and N.Ireland.

At the level of individuals, risks for employed persons were higher than for the unemployed/not in labour force within the different age groups. These differences were larger for females than for males. Differences between risks for employed and unemployed females were clearest for theft of bicycles, personal theft, burglary and all contact crimes.

---

4. More thefts of cars were also reported by women in Finland and Spain, though sampling error could explain this. More car vandalism was reported by women in the USA, though again this difference was not statistically significant. For bicycle theft, risks among women in England & Wales, and Finland were higher, though not statistically significantly. The gender differences reported here are based on risks over five years.

At the national level, 1988 risks among women tended to be more similar to those of men where female employment levels were more equal (r=.410).[5] Highest employment levels for women emerge in Canada, Finland, the USA, England & Wales, and Scotland. With the exception of Finland, these are countries where victimization risks are little related to gender. Lowest levels of female employment are found in Spain, the Netherlands, N.Ireland and Switzerland. The latter three are countries with the largest gender differences in terms of victimization risks.

Overall patterns of reporting to the police

The reporting of crimes to the police was strongly dependent on the type of offence involved, with offences such as theft of cars and motorcycles, and burglary with entry most often reported. The seriousness of crime as a determinant of reporting is in line with results from individual crime surveys, though this does not rule out the possibility that the decision to report may also be influenced by the victims' attitudes towards the police. Reporting rates for individual crimes have already been presented. National overall reporting rates - for all crimes combined - are presented in Figure 33. Figures for offences occurring in 1988 and over the last five years are shown (see also Table E.4). Of those who had been a victim of crime in 1988, 49.6% had reported the last incident to the police. Of those who had been a victim over the last five years, 53.8% had notified the police.[6]

---

5. Countries were rank ordered according to the magnitude of the difference between the victimization rates for males and females (countries with higher rates for females ranking the lowest) and according to the employment rate of females. The Spearman's correlation coefficient was .410. The correlation would have been much stronger if Finland had been left out (a country with high female employment but much higher risks for men). Poland is an example of a country with high female employment where victimization rates of females are slightly higher than those of males. In Indonesia female employment is relatively high too. The victimization rates of females are only slightly lower than those of males. The Polish and Indonesian findings, then, are in line with the hypothesis that victimization by crime is less strongly related to gender where female employment is relatively high.
6. These percentages are based upon the last incident of each type of crime, with the crimes summed. Respondents who had been victimized by more than one type of crime were counted more than once. The 5-year percentages for W.Germany were estimated on the basis of the data about 1988 and of limited data about previous years. In most countries 5-years rates are marginally higher than the 1988 rate. The 5-years rate will be affected by the fact that non-reported incidents are more likely to have been forgotten by respondents, because they tend to be of a less serious nature.

Figure 33: Percentages of crimes reported to the police. Overall percentages for ten different types of crime, 1988 and past five years

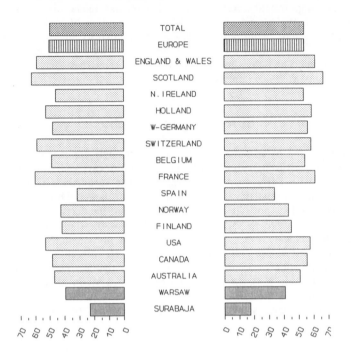

Looking at 5-year figures, the lowest overall reporting rates were found in Surabaja (Indonesia) (18%), and Spain (34%). Other countries with reporting rates below average were Poland (41%), Norway (43%) and Finland (45%). The relatively low overall reporting rates in some countries may indicate a lack of confidence on the part of the public in the efficacy and/or accessibility of their local police.

For all types of crime, reporting was strongly related to the seriousness of the incidents in terms of either injury or value of the stolen/damaged property.[7]

---

7. In all countries for example, reporting of personal thefts was strongly related to the value of stolen property. Of incidents in the highest value quartile, 70% had been reported, compared to 14% of incidents in the lowest quartile (based on data from all countries except Belgium).

68

Reporting to the police was unrelated to gender and age (reporting rates of 1988). Victims in the lowest income group, however, had reported a smaller proportion of their victimization to the police (38%) than those with higher incomes (51%).

The relatively low reporting rate for the lowest income group is partly accounted for by lower mean values of property they had stolen from them, as well as by lower rates of insurance cover (see Chapter 5 for findings on insurance).

Reasons for not reporting

Table 6 combines reasons for non-reporting in relation to the various types of crime covered in the survey. The reasons why the police were not notified do not show much variation internationally. Non-reporting victims in the USA less often mentioned that the crime was not serious enough; they more often mentioned reasons for which a specific coding was not given. In Spain, relatively many victims believed that "the police wouldn't do anything about it", and this may partly explain their rather low reporting rate. In Surabaja (Indonesia), the percentage of non-reporting victims who said they had solved the incident themselves was somewhat higher than in other countries, in accordance with what is believed to happen under custom law traditions. The answers may also reflect, however, a lack of appreciation of the police among respondents not wanting to admit this openly.

Table 6: Reasons for not reporting to the police[1], % mentioning[2]

	theft of car	theft from car	car vanda-lism	theft of motor cycle	theft of bicycle	burg-lary	robber-ry	personal theft	sexual inci-dent	assault/threat
Not serious enough	24.0	43.5	47.0	14.8	5.9	31.0	1.2	38.0	36.8	35.7
Solved it myself	14.7	1.9	3.4	14.8	11.1	15.9	11.1	6.8	19.6	17.2
Inaproppriate for police	4.0	6.5	7.4	7.4	6.3	5.9	6.0	9.3	7.9	8.7
Other authorities	12.0	2.8	2.0	25.9	1.8	7.3	1.2	10.5	3.7	3.8
No insurance	0.0	2.1	1.2	7.4	2.9	1.1	0.2	1.0	0.1	0.1
Police could do nothing	6.7	19.8	25.2	7.4	19.0	16.2	10.9	21.3	8.5	13.2
Police won't do anything	2.7	14.2	10.0	11.1	13.7	7.5	12.0	8.3	6.0	8.9
Fear/dislike police	0.0	0.7	0.3	0.0	0.0	1.7	1.6	0.9	2.6	2.7
Didn't dare	1.3	0.4	0.3	0.0	0.6	0.8	3.5	0.8	4.6	4.8
Other reasons	29.3	16.1	12.1	7.4	20.7	20.7	15.7	17.4	18.6	16.1
Don't know	10.7	5.5	3.9	1.9	2.8	5.0	4.9	2.7	3.8	3.5

1) Based on victims who said they had not reported the last incident of each type to the police.
2) Multiple answers were possible

Satisfaction with the police on reporting

All respondents who reported victimizations to the police in 1988 were asked whether they were satisfied with the way the police dealt with their last report (Figure 34). Two-thirds of the victims were satisfied with the police response; a third (29%) were dissatisfied. Satisfaction among victims was by far the lowest in Warsaw (Poland): only 20% of the victims were satisfied. Relatively low satisfaction was also expressed by victims in Spain, France, Belgium and Norway. Satisfaction was highest in Australia and Canada, and - within Europe - in Finland, the Netherlands, Scotland and England & Wales.

Figure 34: Percentages of victims satisfied with treatment by police

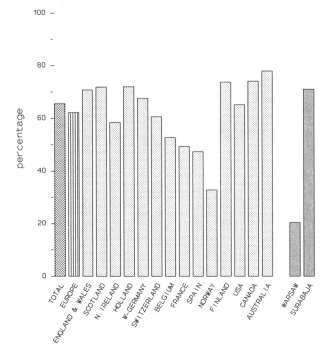

The main reasons for dissatisfaction were that the police "didn't do enough" (42%), were "not interested" (40%), "didn't find the offender" (16%), "didn't recover my property" (17%), "didn't keep me properly informed" (12%), or "didn't treat me correctly" (13%). The numbers are too small to allow detailed comparisons between countries. However, in Warsaw (Poland) relatively many victims complained that the police did not find the offender

(37%) or did not recover the stolen property (50%). In W.Germany, too, relatively many victims complained that the police had not found the offender (30%) or recovered the property (30%). In these countries, victims may have higher expectations as to what the police can accomplish with their investigations.

When victims were unhappy with the police response, this was not clearly related to experience of any particular type of victimization. Though numbers are small (n=32), women who had been sexually assaulted and had reported this to the police were a little more dissatisfied (38% were) than other victims (31% - 35%, depending on offence type). In terms of age, young victims were somewhat more dissatisfied than older ones.

Different types of victims did not vary much in the reasons they gave for being dissatisfied. Victims of sexual assault were more inclined to say the police had not treated them correctly (16%) than others, but as said few sexual assault victims were involved.

General satisfaction with the police

All respondents were asked to give a general judgement on the performance of the police. The question asked was:

"Taken everything into account, how good do you think the police in your area is in controlling crime. Do you think they do a good job or not?".

In all countries, except Warsaw (Poland), a majority of the public felt that the police were doing a good job in controlling crime (Figure 35). General judgement on the police was most favourable in Canada, the USA, Australia, and Indonesia. Apart from Warsaw (Poland), it was least favourable in Switzerland, Spain, and Belgium.

On average only 18% had a negative judgement of police performance and 16% did not feel capable of expressing an opinion. In Warsaw, however, 69% felt the job the police did was not good, and 10% did not express an opinion. This negative judgement may reflect a wider criticism of the police in Warsaw.

Figure 35: Percentage of respondents who think the police are doing a good job in controlling crime in their area

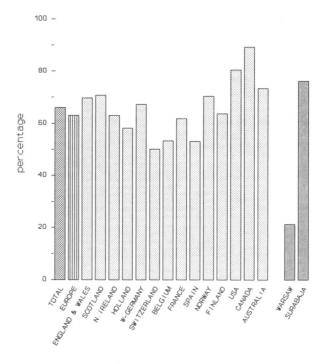

There is no clear relationship between the national levels of victimization and judgements on the police, although at the individual level those who had been victimized in some way in 1988 were more inclined to say the police were not doing a good job (25% did so) than non-victims (16%).

In many countries, younger members of the population were again most critical of police performance.

Victim assistance

Assistance received

Victims in 1988 were asked whether they had been helped by a victim support scheme ("an agency helping victims by giving information, or practical or emotional support"). In most countries, victims are usually referred to victim support agencies by the police. Of victims who had reported one or more crimes in 1988, 3.8% said they had received help.

However, of those who had not reported to the police, 2.3% said they had received help as well. Figure 36 gives the percentages of victims who reported to the police and received help, by country.

Figure 36: Percentage of victims who received specialized help of victims who reported their victimization to the police in 1988

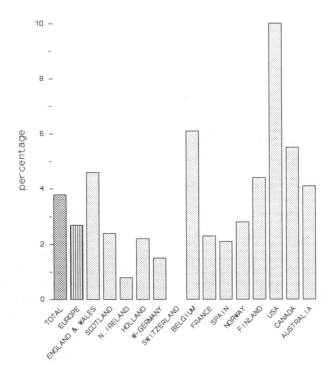

Though the findings must be interpreted with caution since some victims may not have fully understood what was meant by a victim support agency, it appears that relatively many victims received assistance in the USA (10.0%), Belgium, (6.4%), Canada (5.5%), England & Wales (4.6%), and Finland (4.4%).

Table 7 presents the percentages of victims of different types of crime who reported to the police and received help. Those who had reported a sexual

73

incident (15.1%), robbery (8.6%), burglary with entry (7.7%) or an assault/threat (7.3%) were most likely to have been helped.[8]

Table 7: Percentage of victims who in 1988 reported the last crime to the police and who received specialized help from a victim assistance agency, by offence type

Offence		No.
Theft of car	3.3	298
Theft from car	3.4	891
Car vandalism	3.0	707
Theft of motorcycle	-	88
Theft of bicycle	4.1	428
Burglary with entry	7.7	413
Robbery	8.6	129
Personal theft	2.4	445
Sexual incidents	15.1	32
Assaults/threats	7.3	247
Total	3.8	

Apparently, specialized help is most often received by victims of contact crimes and household burglary, the types of victims which are the main targets of assistance agencies in many countries.

A slightly higher percentage of female victims (4.1%) than male victims (3.5%) had received help. Victim aid was also more often received by victims in the two lower income groups (5.8% and 4.6%) than in the higher income groups (3.2% and 3.3%). There was no relationship between age and the use of victim aid.

Those who had received specialized help were somewhat more likely to be very satisfied with their treatment by the police (46%) than whose who did not receive help (30%). On the face of it, this suggests that victims who received help may have appreciated their being referred by the police.

Interest in victim support

Victims who had not received any assistance were asked whether they would have appreciated having it. (The question was: "Looking back at your experiences as a victim, do you feel the services of such an agency would have been useful for you?").

---

8. For those who had been victim of more than one type of crime in 1988 and had reported them all, the data do not show specifically for which crimes assistance had been given. This is unlikely to effect the percentages in Table 7 greatly, though they should not be seen as precise. Victims of less serious crimes who received help, may have received it in relation to a victimization by another crime in the same year.

Opinion about the usefulness of victim aid did not vary a great deal across country: 35% of all victims would have welcomed help (Figure 37). The concept of special services for crime victims, however, was exceptionally popular among victims in Warsaw (Poland), and Surabaja (Indonesia). Victimization by crime may have more serious economic consequences for victims in these two countries. Relatively few victims expressed the need for help in the Netherlands (12%), England & Wales (22%), Scotland (24%) and Canada (24%), though, as shown, in some of these countries assistance was more likely to be given.

It is clear that, in all countries, a much larger group of victims would have appreciated assistance than have actually got it.

Figure 37: Percentage of victims in 1988 who said the services of a victim assistance scheme would have been useful for them

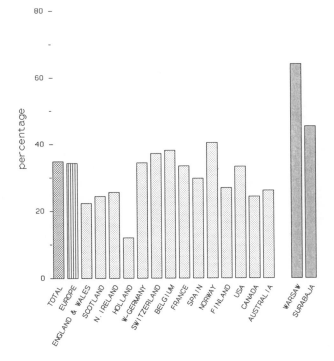

Victims expressing interest in victim support do not match the stereotype of the vulnerable elderly lady: there was little relationship between the demand for support and either gender, age or level of income.

The demand for victim support was highest among victims of sexual incidents (62% said they would have liked help), and those who had been threatened/assaulted (47%).[9] Of those who had been threatened 52% would have appreciated help. This finding suggests that many of the reported threats have been quite frightening.

Among victims of robbery, 38% said they would have liked support, and 34% of those who had experienced burglary with entry. A rather larger proportion of those who had bicycles stolen (45%) were in favour of support, but some victims of such thefts may have interpreted victim support as offering financial compensation for stolen property. The demand for support was lower among victims of theft of cars (27%), but they may have been more extensively covered by insurance.

---

9. For those who had been victim of more than one type of crime in 1988 the data do not show specifically for which crime they would have appreciated help.

4 Responses to crime

Fear of crime

Street crime

Respondents were asked whether to avoid crime the last time they went out after dark in their area, they had (i) stayed away from certain streets or areas, and (ii) had gone accompanied by someone else. The measure aims to tap levels of fear about victimization by violent crime in public places - for simplicity 'street crime'. In the analysis below, those who had done neither of these things are separated from those who had done one of them, or both.

Fear of street crime is highest in W.Germany, England & Wales and the USA. It is relatively low in N.Ireland, Norway, Finland and Canada (see Figure 38). Fear was very high in Warsaw (Poland) and Surabaja (Indonesia), though this will be partly explained by their being urban centres.

Precautionary measures are, of course, not relevant for those who never go out after dark, and indeed fear of crime itself may be one reason for not going our (infirmity will be another). However, in countries where fear as measured was highest people did not consistently stay in after dark most often: the highest figures for those who never went out were in Spain (13.7%), England & Wales (12.9%), Scotland (9.8%) and France (9.4%) - not necessarily countries where fear was highest. On average, 6.4% of people said they never went out after dark.

Figure 38: Fear of street crime. Percentage of people who take one or two precautionary measures when going out to avoid crime

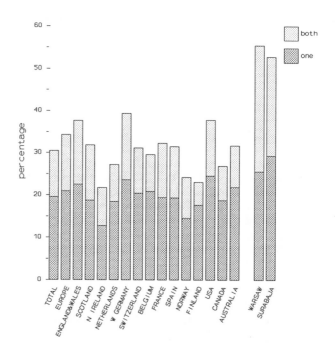

Fear was much higher among women than among men, and also higher among inhabitants of larger cities (Table 8). Among women, an overall 24.6% took one measure and 17.3% both; the figures for men were 14.2% and 4.0%. In W.Germany and England & Wales, more than half of women had taken at least one measure (57.3% and 51.5% respectively). Figures were also high in Warsaw (Poland) and Surabaja (Indonesia) - though as said these are urban locations.

Persons below 35 years of age - women in particular - are more likely to take precautions when going out than others. The relatively low number of the elderly who took precautionary measures is largely accounted for by the high proportion who said they never went out in the evening at all (ranging from 10% to 20% in various countries). The elderly may stay at home because they feel unsafe out of doors at night, though other reasons are as likely to restrict their mobility.

Table 8: Fear of street crime of different population groups in fourteen countries. Percentage taking precautionary measures

	None %	One %	Two %	N
Sex				
Male	81.8	14.2	4.0	13,542
Female	58.1	24.6	17.3	14,458
Age				
16-34	65.8	20.9	13.3	10,716
35-54	71.1	18.9	10.0	9,047
55+	72.7	18.6	8.7	8,139
Size of place of residence (1)				
<10,000	78.0	14.0	8.0	9,317
10,000-50,000	71.6	18.3	10.1	6,408
>50,000	59.4	26.3	14.3	8,490

1. Excludes respondents who did not know size of place of residence.

As measured here, fear of street crime appears to be wholly unrelated to national victimization rates for crimes of violence. Nonetheless, women who reported having been a victim of a sexual incident or assault/threat in the past five years were more likely to take precautions when going out at night: for example, 30% of those who were victim of both crimes took both precautions, 25% of those who had experienced one of the offences, and 16% of those not victimized. Precautionary behaviour, however, was far from confined to victims alone: nearly 90% of the women who adopted both measures had not experienced any assaultive behaviour in the past five years.

The findings, then, indicate that precautionary behaviour is determined by factors other than simply exposure to violent crime as measured by the survey. In Surabaja, for instance, it is customary for older women to be always escorted by a younger family member when going out. In other countries, extensive mass media portrayal of violent crime may inspire readers or viewers to take precautions.

Burglary

A question was put to respondents to probe their perceptions of the likelihood of household burglary:

"What would you say are the chances that over the next twelve months someone will try to break into your home? Do you think this is very likely, likely or not likely?"

Concern that a burglary was likely or very likely to happen in the next year was highest among those in W.Germany (54%), Switzerland (46%) and Australia (44%). Least troubled were those in Finland and Norway. Figure 39 shows details.

Within most countries, concern about burglary was higher in larger cities. In line with this, 77% of people in Warsaw (Poland) thought themselves vulnerable to a burglary in the coming year.

Not surprisingly, those who reported having been burgled in 1988 saw their risk of having another burglary as greater (51%) than those who had not had a break-in (32%).

Figure 39: Percentage of respondents thinking burglary very likely or likely to them the next year

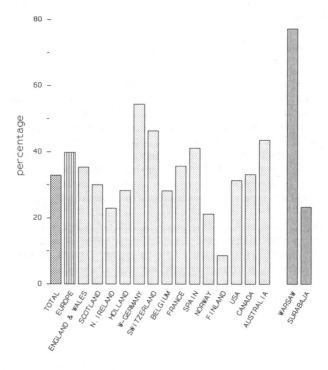

Unlike fear of street crime, perceptions of the risk of burglary were strongly related to national burglary rates. Countries where high proportions thought they would be very likely to be a victim tended to be those with higher burglary risks (r=.834; see Figure 40).

Figure 40: Victimization rates of burglary (including attempts) in the last five years by percentage of respondents who thought it very likely they would be burgled in the next year

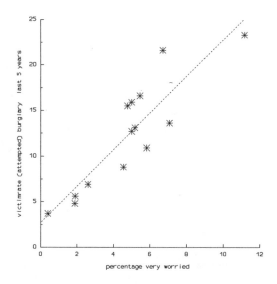

Attitudes to punishment

One question was put to respondents about their opinions on sentencing. They were asked which of five types of sentences they considered to be the most appropriate for a recidivist burglar ("A man of 21 years old who is found guilty of burglary for the second time. This time he stole a colour TV"). The selected sentences were: a fine, imprisonment, community service, a suspended sentence, or some other sentence. Table 9 presents the percentage of respondents opting for either a fine, prison or a community service order.

Table 9: Percentage in favour of a fine, a prison sentence or community service order for a recidivist burglar

	fine	prison	community service
Total	12.9	27.5	41.2
Europe	12.7	22.2	45.2
England & Wales	11.4	38.2	37.5
Scotland	14.4	39.0	33.5
N.Ireland	9.0	45.4	30.2
Netherlands	9.2	25.6	46.0
W.Germany	8.8	13.0	60.0
Switzerland	11.6	8.6	56.7
Belgium	13.2	25.5	37.7
France	10.3	12.8	53.0
Spain	23.4	27.0	23.4
Norway	23.0	13.8	47.0
Finland	18.9	15.0	36.8
USA	8.2	52.7	29.6
Canada	10.7	32.5	39.2
Australia	8.5	35.6	45.7
Warsaw	4.6	42.4	37.8
Surabaja	1.5	66.5	5.7

Contrary to conventional wisdom, imprisonment is generally not the public's preferred punishment for a recidivist burglar. In most countries, the majority favoured other sentences. However, in Surabaja (Indonesia) a full 67% favoured imprisonment, and in the USA slightly more than half did so (53%). These aside, imprisonment was relatively popular in Warsaw (Poland) (42%), Australia (36%), and Canada (33%). The same was true of all countries in the United Kingdom (England & Wales (38%), Scotland (39%) and N.Ireland (45%), suggesting a special British tradition of punishment by means of imprisonment.

In all countries except the USA, support for prison sentences was lowest among people with a high level of education (those who left school at 20 years of age or later).

Preference for imprisonment was slightly stronger among victims: 36% of those who had a burglar in their home in 1988 opted for imprisonment, 33% of those victimized over the last five years, and 27% of non-victims. In parallel with this, countries with the highest burglary risks were more likely to recommend imprisonment for the burglar.[1]

Respondents who favoured imprisonment were asked how long the burglar should go to prison. Those in countries where imprisonment was preferred

---

1. r=.572; p<0.05; five-year risks. The figure was similar for those who were victims of burglary in 1988.

also tended to favour a relatively long sentence. A prison sentence of one year or more was recommended most often by those in Warsaw (95%), Surabaja (80%), and the USA (73%); these figures compare with an average figure of 46% of people recommending such a sentence.

Public opinion and imprisonment rates

The percentage of respondents in each country favouring a prison sentence were compared with Council of Europe and other statistics on the number of prisoners per 100,000 inhabitants in 1988 (Figure 41). Prisoner rates seem broadly to reflect public attitudes towards sentences, with highest per capita imprisonment generally matching support for imprisonment as the best sentencing option (r=.610).

Although support for imprisonment was strong in the USA, actual imprisonment rates are very much higher than in other countries. In the Netherlands the imprisonment rate is the lowest (36 per 100,000), while support for imprisonment is moderate.

Imprisonment rates in Poland as a whole were also extremely high (265 per 100,000 population in 1988; Bienkovska, 1989), against moderately strong support for imprisonment among respondents in Warsaw. There was greater support for imprisonment in Surabaja, but according to the available statistics national imprisonment rates were only moderate (19 per 100,000 population; Biles, 1987). Data for Poland and Indonesia are not shown in Figure 41.

Figure 41: Prisoners per 100,000 population, by percentage of respondents who would give a burglar a prison sentence if caught for the second time

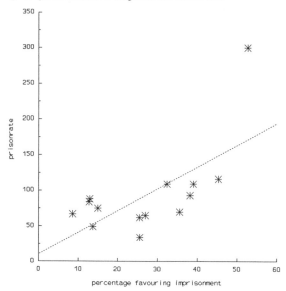

83

Community service orders

Within Europe as a whole, the public considered a community service order to be the most appropriate punishment for a recidivist burglar. Those in W.Germany (60%), Switzerland (57%) and France (53%) were particularly in favour of this sanction. In Spain, Norway and Finland a fine was also a relatively popular option: about one in five people recommended this.

Again in most countries, the well-educated were significantly more supportive of community service orders. This result is in line with findings of studies in a number of countries that the better educated public are more in favour of less punitive sanctions and of a preventive approach to the problems of crime generally (eg. Robert and Faugeron, 1978; Walker et al., 1988; Van Dijk and Steinmetz, 1988; Boers and Sessar, 1988; Brillon, 1988; Killias, 1989).

Among those who had been burgled (either in 1988 or over the past five years), a community service order was the most favoured sentencing option, with four out of ten victims supporting this. Burglary victims were just as likely to support community service as non-victims.

5 Crime prevention measures

Crime prevention

Information was gathered about protection against household crime, in particular burglary. Respondents were asked whether (i) a caretaker was employed where they lived (though only for those living in apartments (or 'flats'); (ii) a burglar alarm was fitted; (iii) lights were kept on when the house was empty (as an occupancy proxy); and (iv) neighbours were asked to keep an eye on things if the household was away for a day or two.

There are two main ways in which security precautions and risks might be associated. First, if risks of burglary are high this might convince people of the need to take precautions, in which case a positive relationship between risks and protection would be expected. Or, if precautions are routinely taken by a large proportion of the population this could reduce overall risks, thus giving a negative relationship. In reality, the relationship might be more complex. People who are security conscious might possibly reduce their own risks, but if sufficient numbers of other people are more lax about security, overall burglary risks might nonetheless be high because of the easy opportunities given to potential offenders. In any event, it is unlikely that any simple, clear relationship between risks and precautions will be apparent at national level.

As a further point, it should be borne in mind that some respondents may have exaggerated the precautions they took against burglary. Principally, this might have been because of some residual mistrust about the credentials of the survey, and a reluctance to admit to unknown interviewers that the home was less protected than it might be. Since reactions among respondents varied considerably between different countries with regard to their reaction to the household security questions, the differences in precautions discussed below may partly reflect differential wariness rather than 'real' differences in security habits. This should be borne in mind.

Caretakers

Overall, about a quarter of all respondents lived in apartments (28%), with the highest figures being in Spain (67%), Switzerland (64%), W.Germany (48%), France (35%) and Finland (36%).

Caretakers were quite common in apartment buildings in the USA, Canada and Australia, though only a minority of people lived in them. Within Europe, caretakers were relatively common in Finland, France, Norway, and Belgium. Relatively few caretakers were employed in Switzerland, the Netherlands and Scotland. Figure 42 shows details.

Figure 42: Percentages of flats or apartments which have a caretaker

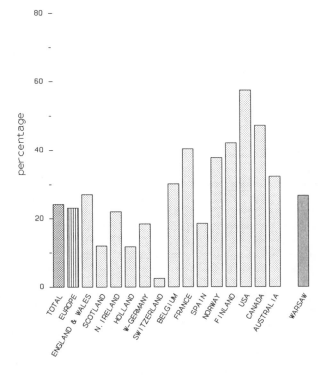

The employment of caretakers is currently being promoted as a crime prevention measure - for instance, in England & Wales and the Netherlands - on the basis of evidence that the surveillance they provide can reduce burglary risks (Hesseling, 1989; Waller and Okihiro, 1978; Reppetto, 1974). At the national level of analysis, the results do not suggest any consistent association between the use of caretakers and risks of burglary with entry.

Looking at individual householders, risks in 1988 were somewhat higher for those flats with caretakers (2.2%) than those without (1.7%). This may be because caretakers tend to be employed in high risk areas in particular. However, in some countries where caretakers are more common - such as

France, Belgium and Canada - flats with a so-called 'concierge' system have much lower risks than those without[1].

In general, risks of attempted burglary in 1988 were also higher in flats with caretakers, and indeed the difference in risks was more pronounced than for burglary with entry. Thus, 3.1% of those in flats with caretakers had experienced an attempted burglary, compared with 1.8% of those in other flats; or put another way, 60% of burglaries against those with caretakers were unsuccessful, as against 49%, against others.

In sum then, the evidence is mixed as to the effectiveness of caretakers. In some countries risks are higher for those in flats with caretakers, through this may be due to high risk location. In other countries - were caretakers are more common - risks are lower in flats with a 'concierge'. There is also a suggestion that more burglaries may be prevented from being successful where there is a caretaker present.

Burglar alarms

The use of a burglar alarm is particularly relevant for those living in terraced, semi-detached or detached houses. The percentage of such houses protected by a burglar alarm varied widely between the participating countries (see Figure 43). In Finland, Spain, Belgium and Switzerland, few houses had such protection. Alarms were much more common in England & Wales, Scotland, W.Germany and in the non-European countries - though it should be borne in mind, as mentioned above, that some respondents may have falsely said they had an alarm.[2]

In most countries, alarms were more often installed by more affluent households, and those living in larger cities (both groups of the population with above average burglary risks).

---

1. In France the percentages were 1.9% (with a concierge) and 3.8% (without) - N=214; N=317. In Belgium, the figures were 1.0% and 3.0% (N=100; N=231). In Canada, the figures were 1.8% and 5.4% (N=165; N=186).
2. Other estimates of alarm ownership in England & Wales and the USA at least, are lower - much lower in the case of England & Wales - than the present figures.

Figure 43: Percentage of terraced, semi-detached or detached houses protected by a burglar alarm

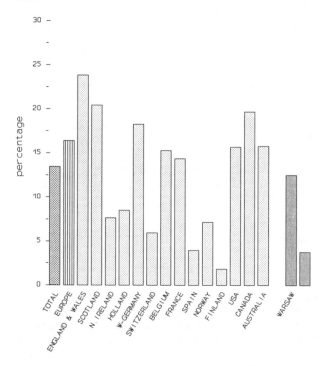

As Figure 44 shows, the use of alarms appears to be moderately related to the national rate of victimization for burglary, such that higher alarm rates are associated with *higher* risks of burglary, including attempts (r=.574). There are several exceptions. In Australia and the USA the rates of burglar alarms are moderately high (16%), but burglary rates of these two countries are the highest (including attempts 23.7% and 21.6%). In W.Germany, the rate of burglary alarms is rather high (18%), but the burglary rate is low (8.8%).

Looking at the individual householders, 14.6% of those with alarms had a burglary over five years, as against 7.1% of those without. There is no simple interpretation of this statistical relationship. Households who see themselves as most vulnerable to burglary are likely to install alarms as protection, while those who had experienced a burglary may well have got an alarm as a direct result. More focused research is needed to assess whether alarm ownership reduces risk.

From the present data there is some suggestion that alarm owners were more likely to experience attempted burglary than non-owners: 57% of incidents against alarm owners were unsuccessful (n=171), as against 46% of those against other households (n=678). A similar finding has also emerged in other research (eg, Hough and Mo, 1986; Killias, 1989).

Figure 44: Percentage of terraced, semi-detached and detached houses protected by a burglar alarm, by five year victimization rates for burglary, including attempts

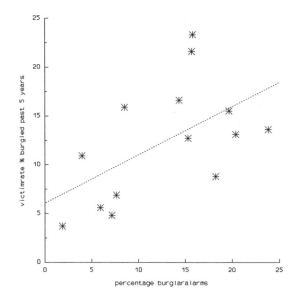

Lighting

Keeping lights on when the home is empty in the evening appeared either a very common habit, or one which few householders adopted (Figure 45).

Figure 45: Percentage of householders who keep lights on when their home is left empty in the evening

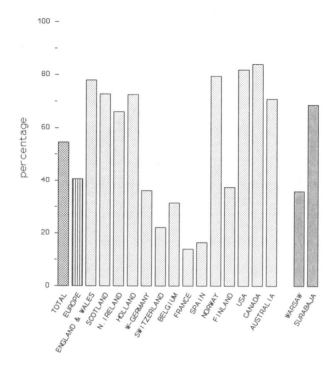

In countries where it was common to keep lights on, about 70% of those who said they did this claimed to *always* do it. When it was less common to leave lights on, the proportion of people who always did it was much lower (between 38% and 47%). Leaving lights on was less common in countries with relatively few semi-detached or detached houses, such as Spain, Switzerland, W.Germany, France, Finland, and Surabaja.

The use of lights tended to be more common in countries where national burglary risk were higher, though the relationship was statistically weak (r=0.174; ns).

At the individual level, risks of burglary with entry in 1988 were also higher in nearly all countries for those who keep their lights on (2.6% on average) than for those who do not (1.4%). Differences in risks of attempted burglary were similar (2.5% for those using lights and 1.4% for others). Since other factors may influence these results, no firm inference can be drawn about the effectiveness of 'keeping the lights on' as an anti-burglary measure. The data suggest, however, that the deterrent value of keeping the house well-lit would be limited. This finding is in line with research on the perception of burglars. Timed automatic interior lights were rated as one of the least effective crime prevention measures by experienced burglars in the USA (Figgie, 1988). Dutch burglars have even indicated that they interpret single lights being on as a sign that the house is empty (Korthals Altes and Van Soomeren, 1989).

Surveillance by neighbours

Another precautionary measure against burglary is to ask a neighbour or a caretaker to watch the home when it is left empty. In most countries, a majority of householders do this, exceptions being Spain, Finland and Norway (see Figure 46).

Of all respondents, 13.2% said they had not asked for any surveillance, because it was done anyway. It might be argued that these respondents benefit from a kind of 'natural surveillance', due to a favourable design of their houses, the presence of a caretaker, or a close existing community spirit. It is also possible that surveillance was not asked for because it already took place under a Neighbourhood Watch or Blockwatch scheme (though routinely asking for surveillance is considered an essential part of such schemes). In any event, such 'natural surveillance' was relatively common in W.Germany (20.3%), Norway (20%), England & Wales (17%), and Scotland (15.9%). It was less common in the USA (5.6%) and Canada (7.6%).

Asking for neighbours to help was more likely in countries with the higher burglary risks, though again not very strongly (r=.226; ns).

At the level of individual householders, the results for all 14 countries combined do not support the idea that people who ask neighbours for help in watching their home have lower burglary risks. This is no doubt because these householders are reacting to a realistic appreciation of their existing higher risks. Thus, overall, 8.9% of those who had asked for surveillance had experienced a burglary with entry over the past five years, while risks were lower for both houses with 'natural surveillance' (6.4%) and those without any kind of surveillance (6.6%). Similarly, risks of attempted burglary were highest for those who asked for surveillance (7.6%), and lower for those with 'natural surveillance' (6.0%), and those who had not asked for help (5.3%). As a corollary, there was no evidence that asking for surveillance made any difference to the proportion of burglaries which were successful, or not.

However, these overall results conceal the fact that in most countries - Switzerland, Finland, the USA and Spain were exceptions - owners in houses with 'natural surveillance' had lower risks of burglary than those who did not. In the Netherlands, for instance, risks of burglary with entry among those in houses with 'natural surveillance' was 3.4% (n=256). It was 9.7% for those who had asked for surveillance (n=1170) and 9.9% for those who had not (n=518). In England & Wales, the comparable figures were 7.0%, 9.4% and 10.0% respectively (n=340; 1348; 287).

These findings again, then, indicate that people who ask neighbours for help in watching their home do not necessarily enjoy lower burglary risks, though this should not be unexpected. They do, however, suggest that in some countries at least those with the benefit of 'natural surveillance' may experience lower risks. This may be because of surveillance per se, because of good housing design, or because helpful neighbours are an inherent feature of communities in which burglary risks are low.

Figure 46: Percentage of householders who ask a neighbour or caretaker to watch their house when it is empty for a day or two

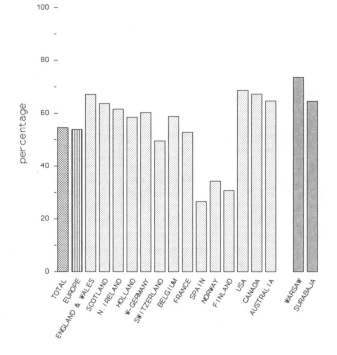

Insurance

Respondents were asked whether their house was insured against burglary. Insurance rates were highest in Switzerland, Scotland, England & Wales, and the Netherlands. They were very low in Surabaja (Indonesia) - 2% - and relatively low in Belgium and Spain. Figure 47 shows details.

Figure 47: Percentages of houses insured against burglary

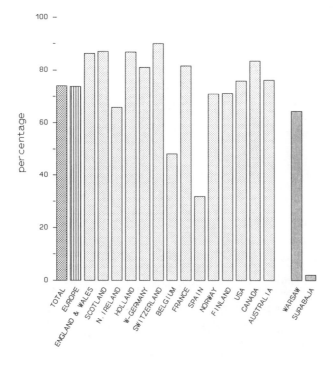

As has been discussed earlier, rates of reporting burglary to the police tend to be somewhat lower in countries where relatively few households have insurance cover. Amongst individual victims too, insurance is related to the reporting of burglaries to the police (see Chapter 2). Fewer households with a below average income level have insurance cover. This partly accounts for the relatively low reporting rate of the lowest income group (see Chapter 3).

Gun ownership

Respondents were asked whether they or someone else in their household owned a gun. Ownership rates for handguns and rifles varied between 2% in the Netherlands to 49% in the USA. Possession of rifles was more common in rural areas. The ownership of handguns is criminologically more relevant than ownership of rifles. Figure 48 presents national ownership rates for handguns.

Figure 48: Percentages of households with handguns

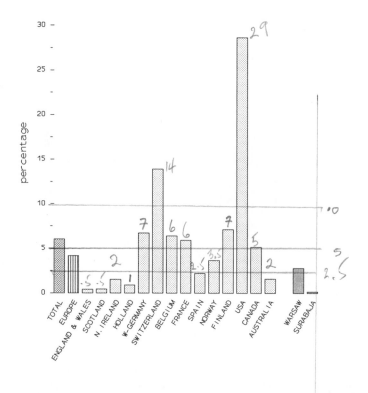

The possession of handguns is by far the most common in the USA (29%). In Europe, relatively high rates are found in Switzerland (14%), Finland (7%), W.Germany (7%), Belgium (6%) and France (6%). In Switzerland most handguns are owned by men in their capacity as members of the army: 52% of all handguns were said to be army guns.

At the individual level the possession of handguns is more common among males and among households with an above average income.

94

6 Summary and conclusions

This report has presented results from an international research project in which surveys were conducted with representative samples of national populations of people aged 16 years or more about their experiences of crime. The surveys took place in the early part of 1989. Fourteen countries, in and out of Europe, conducted surveys which were fully standardized as regards sampling method, method of interview, and questions asked. Surveys were also conducted in Japan, and in the cities of Warsaw (Poland) and Surabaja (East Java, Indonesia), although with some differences in survey techniques. This report concentrates mainly on results from the fourteen major participating countries, though results from Indonesia and Poland get some mention. Results from Japan are not yet available.

The survey was based on well-tried techniques of measuring crime and crime-related issues used in surveys which have been independently mounted in a number of countries. However, results from these surveys are extremely difficult to compare because of differences in survey administration and data analysis. The present survey, which used the same questionnaire and sampling techniques in all main participating countries, provides much more strictly comparable information.

Fieldwork was carried out almost entirely through computer assisted telephone interviewing (CATI). Technical organization of survey was the responsibility of Inter/View of Amsterdam who subcontracted fieldwork in different countries to affiliated companies. The study was commissioned by the governments of the participating countries at the invitation of a Working Group, consisting of Jan J.M. van Dijk (Ministry of Justice, the Netherlands, general coordinator), Pat Mayhew (Home Office, UK) and Martin Killias (University of Lausanne, Switzerland).

The survey provides unique comparative information about people's experience of crime. It gives a measure of the extent of criminal victimization which is independent of that based on statistics of offences recorded by the police. These statistics enumerate only crimes reported to, and recorded by the police, and have been found difficult to use for comparative purposes. The survey also collected from respondents in each country comparative information about their responses to crime.

Summary

This report is intended to give an overview of the key findings of the survey. These are summarized below. Where victimization risks are mentioned, these are based on the percentage of respondents in the sample who said they had been victimized once or more in 1988, unless otherwise specified. The findings on risks from the local surveys in Warsaw (Poland) and Surabaja (Indonesia) are presented under a separate heading.

Offences against vehicles

- The risk of having a car stolen in 1988 was highest in France (2.3%), Australia (2.3%), the USA (2.1%), and England & Wales (1.8%). These relatively high rates are in part accounted for by high levels of car ownership, though even taking ownership differences into account relative risks were similar.
- Thefts of motorcycles/mopeds/scooters were highest in Switzerland (1.2%), Spain (0.8%) and France (0.6%). These are matched by high ownership levels, though again taking ownership into account relative risks were similar. Over the past five years, 17% of owners in France had a motorcycle stolen, and 16% in Switzerland.
- Thefts of bicycles in 1988 was by far the highest in the Netherlands (7.6%). Relatively high rates were also found in Canada (3.4%), W.Germany (3.3%), Switzerland (3.2%), the USA (3.1%), and Finland (3.1%). In all these countries, bicycle ownership is relatively common, though risk patterns for owners are similar, being particularly high in the Netherlands.
- In 1988, risks of thefts from cars (luggage, radios, car mirrors etc.) were highest in Spain (9.9%), the USA (9.3%), Canada (7.2%), and Australia (6.9%). Those in Switzerland, Belgium, Finland, and Norway faced relatively low risks. For owners in Europe, risks were relatively high in Scotland, England & Wales, France and the Netherlands.
- Damage to cars was most common in Canada (9.8%), Australia (8.7%), W.Germany (8.7%) and the USA (8.9%). Low risks were found in Finland, Switzerland, N.Ireland and Norway.
- The high risks of theft from cars and car vandalism in the USA, Canada and Australia are partly accounted for by high car ownership in these countries.

Opportunity and vehicle-related offences

- In general, countries with higher rates of ownership of vehicles of different kinds had higher levels of offences involving these vehicles. Not only overall risks, but also risks for owners were higher in countries with higher ownership levels. These findings suggest that one determinant of the amount of vehicle crime is the availability of targets to steal. In countries where vehicles are common the *demand* for targets is higher. Vehicle crime seems to be sustained by plentiful targets, rather than caused by few vehicles being available to the population generally.

- In countries where car thefts were low, bicycle thefts were high: many offenders who steal because of the need for temporary transportation appear to make do with a bicycle, if there are enough of them around.

Burglary

- Burglars got into the home most often in 1988 in Australia (4.4%), USA (3.8%) and Canada (3.0%). Within Europe, highest risks were faced by those in France (2.4%), the Netherlands (2.4%) and Belgium (2.3%). Low risks were found in Norway, Finland and Switzerland.
- Risks of attempted burglary were also highest in the USA, Australia and Canada. Attempts were relatively common in the Netherlands and France, though not particularly so in England & Wales and Scotland.
- Rates of burglary with entry differed by type of dwelling: 8.6% of detached and semi-detached houses were burgled over five years, as against 7% of flats and terraced houses. Within individual countries, however, housing type was not consistently related to burglary risk. In the USA, for instance, risks were the highest for flats, but in Australia for detached or semi-detached houses. The high burglary risk in Australia may be possibly related to the high proportion (85%) of Australian houses which are detached or semi-detached.

Robbery

- Robbery was most common in 1988 in Spain (2.8%) and the USA (1.9%). In 40% of incidents in Spain, the offender used a knife, compared to 20% on average. In the USA, 28% of offenders used a gun, compared to 8% on average.
- The high percentage of gun-point robberies in the USA corresponds with survey findings on gun ownership. The ownership of handguns was much more common in the USA (29%) than elsewhere (average 6%). Other countries with relatively high percentages of handgun owners were Switzerland (14%), Finland (7%), W.Germany (7%), Belgium (6%) and France (6%). In Switzerland, just over half of handguns were said to be army guns.

Thefts of personal property including pickpocketing

- The 1988 victimization rates for non-violent thefts of personal property were highest in Canada (5.4%), Spain (5.0%) and Australia (5.0%).

- A sub-category of personal thefts was *pickpocketing*. Risks were markedly higher in Spain (2.8%), and were generally low outside Europe (in the USA, Australia and Canada). Women were more vulnerable than men.

Sexual incidents

- Only women were asked about sexual incidents. Women reported such incidents most often in the three non-European countries: among women in Australia, 7.3% reported a sexual incident, 4.5% in the USA, and 4.0% in Canada. In Europe, risks were highest in W.Germany (2.8%), the Netherlands (2.6%) and Spain (2.4%). These results must be interpreted with caution, since readiness to talk about such experiences may vary across culture. Of the incidents described, 3% were said to be actual rapes, 9% attempted rape, 17% indecent assaults and 69% 'offensive behaviour'.
- Sexual assaults (rape, attempted rape, and indecent assault) were highest in the USA (2.3% of women reported an assault in 1988), Canada (1.7%), Australia (1.6%) and W.Germany (1.5%).

Assaults/threats

- Incidents involving assaults and frightening threats were highest in 1988 in the three non-European countries: the USA (5.4%), Australia (5.2%), and Canada (4.0%). Within Europe, they were highest in the Netherlands (3.4%), W.Germany (3.1%), Spain (3.0%), Norway (3.0%), and Finland (2.9%). In general, national findings on sexual violence and on threats/assaults appear similar.
- Assaults actually involving force were most common against Australians (3%) and those in the USA (2.3%). Within Europe, risks were highest in the Netherlands (2.0%) and Finland (2.0%), the latter a country with generally low risks of other crime.

Overall victimization

- The prevalence victimization rate for all crimes in 1988 was highest in the USA (28.8%). High rates were also found in Canada (28.1%) and Australia (27.8%). Among the participating European countries, the highest rates were in the Netherlands (26.8%), Spain (24.6%) and W.Germany (21.9%). The lowest rates were found in Norway (16.5%), Finland (15.9%), Switzerland (15.6%), and N.Ireland (15.0%).
- The overall prevalence victimization rates for five years were highest in the Netherlands (60.4%), the USA (57.6%), Australia (57.2%), Canada (53%), France (52%), Spain (51.6%) and W.Germany (51.3%). The high Dutch rate is partly due to the very high victimization rate for bicycle theft (25%).

- The picture from an incidence measure of all crimes in 1988 reported by respondents was very similar to that from the prevalence measure above (percentage of respondents who reported one victimization or more). Highest incidence risks were found in the USA (62.1 crimes per 100 respondents), Australia (58.7) and Canada (48.1). In Europe, highest incidence risks were in the Netherlands (46.9), Spain (47.5), and W.Germany (37.7). On an incidence measure, the total number of crimes people experienced is taken into account.

Rates of victimization in cities

- Victimization rates in cities of more than 100,000 inhabitants were generally higher in the USA than elsewhere, though there are exceptions for some crimes. Rates in cities in Canada and W.Europe are not greatly dissimilar. Australian city rates are somewhat variable across crime, but generally below those of the USA and Canada.

Victimization rates in Warsaw (Poland) and Surabaja (East Java/Indonesia)

- Polish and Indonesian rates were compared with those of cities of more than 100,000 inhabitants in the USA, Canada, W.Europe and Australia. Rates in Warsaw resemble W.European rates, although thefts of personal property - in particular pickpocketing - are more common. Rates in Surabaja are lower for car-related crimes, on account of a much lower ownership rate. The rate for assault/threats in Surabaja is also very low.

Circumstances of victimization

- Of all the offences measured, nearly half had taken place near the victim's own home, and a third elsewhere in the city or local area. Roughly one in ten offences took place elsewhere in the country.
- 4% of incidents happened abroad. However, the Swiss were particularly prone to offences abroad: 16% of incidents against them took place outside Switzerland. The proportion of incidents abroad was also relatively high for those from Finland (9%), W.Germany (8%) and Belgium (8%). Figures of crime risk for these countries therefore somewhat overstate local vulnerability.

Who is at risk?

- For most types of crime the young tend to be more at risk than the elderly, men more than women, and city dwellers more than inhabitants of rural areas or small towns. Those who go out most often in the evening for recreational purposes have higher risks of all offences.

- Victimization rates in general are higher among those with above-average incomes.
- Risks among women tended to be more similar to those of men where female employment levels were more equal, such as in the USA and Poland. In countries with low levels of female employment, such as the Netherlands, N.Ireland and Switzerland, victimization risks for women are substantially lower than those for men.
- Countries with the lowest crime are characterized by a relatively low level of urbanization, ie. many of their inhabitants live in small villages and relatively few in cities with 100,000 inhabitants or more.

Survey estimates and police figures

- The ranking of survey levels of victimization for five types of crimes was compared with the ranking of offences recorded by the police in different countries. There is far from close correspondence between the two measures, but similarity on various fronts. The closest association was between the two measures of thefts of cars, an offence particularly likely to be reported to the police. Burglary levels were moderately associated. For robbery, assault and sexual offences, there was poor correspondence. However, correspondence was fairly strong when only survey crimes reported to the police were considered.
- These results suggest that for comparative purposes survey victimization rates may well be a more valid measure of the burden of crime upon the public than police statistics, since they are less affected by differences in reporting and/or official recording.

Reporting to the police

- The percentage of crimes reported to the police in 1988 differs by crime type. Taking figures for the main 14 participating countries, some property crimes have relatively higher reporting rates: eg. car theft (93%), burglary (77%), and bicycle theft (60%). Robbery has a lower reporting rate (49%), as do personal thefts (41%), assaults (31%) and car vandalism (39%). Sexual incidents were least likely to be reported (10%), but the reporting of sexual assaults and rape was higher (24% and 48%, respectively).
- For all crimes measures in the survey, an average of 50% were reported to the police (1988 rate).
- Overall reporting percentages over five years were very low in Indonesia (18%) and relatively low in Spain (34%), Poland (41%), Norway (43%) and Finland (45%).
- Those within the lowest income group, had reported a smaller percentage (38%) of their victimizations to the police than others (51%).
- Those who said they had no insurance cover against burglary were less likely to report burglaries to the police (65%) than others (87%).

100

Similarly, countries with a relatively low proportion of households with insurance cover had lower reporting rates.

- The main reasons given by victims for not reporting were that the incident was: "not serious enough" (40%), that the "police could do nothing" (19%) and that "police won't do anything" (10%). This pattern was generally consistent across country.
- When they reported to the police, most victims were satisfied with the way they were dealt with (66%). A relatively low level of satisfaction was expressed by victims in Poland (20%), Norway (33%), Spain (47%), France (49%), and Belgium (53%).
- The main reasons why victims were dissatisfied were that the "police didn't do enough" (41%), or "were not interested (41%).

Other attitudes to the police

- Two-thirds of the public felt that the police were doing a good job in controlling crime in their area. Highest levels of satisfaction with local police performance were in Canada (89%), USA (81%), Surabaja (76%), and Australia (73%).
- Dissatisfaction with police performance was highest in Poland (69% thought they did a poor job); it was also relatively high in Spain (29%), W.Germany (24%), and Belgium (22%).
- Satisfaction with the police did not appear to be related to overall country levels of crime, though victims (25%) were unhappier about the police than non-victims were (16%).

Victim support

- Only 3.8% of victims who reported crimes to the police received any help from an agency specializing in giving information or practical or emotional support to crime victims. This percentage was higher in the USA (10.0%), Belgium (6.4%), Canada (5.5%), England & Wales (4.0%), and Finland (4.4%).
- Those who had reported a sexual incident (15.1%), a robbery (8.6%), a burglary (7.7%) or a threat/assault (7.3%) were most likely to have received specialized help.
- Help had more often been received by female victims (4.1%) and by victims with a below average income (5.8% of those in the lowest income group had received help).
- In all countries, a much larger group of victims would have appreciated assistance than actually got it. In all, 35% of victims said that services of a support agency would have been useful for them. The figure was particularly high in Indonesia (74%) and Poland (63%).
- The demand for victim support was highest among victims of sexual incidents and threats/assault. There was little relationship between the demand for support and either gender or age.

Fear of crime

- Fear of street crime was measured by two questions about precautionary behaviour. As measured, fear is highest in W.Germany, England & Wales and the USA, as well as in Warsaw and Surabaja. Fear is unrelated to national victimization rates for crimes of violence. Precautionary behaviour seems to be determined by factors other than exposure to violent crime.
- Women were much more likely to take precautionary measures against street crime than men. Those who have been a victim of a crime of violence are also more likely to take precautions.
- Concern about burglary was highest in W.Germany, Switzerland and Australia. Unlike fear of street crime, perceptions of the risk of burglary were generally related to national burglary rates.
- Within most countries, concern about burglary was higher amongst those who had been burgled in 1988.

Attitudes to punishment

- All respondents were asked what would be the most appropriate sentence for a recidivist burglar aged 21. Contrary to conventional wisdom, imprisonment is generally not the public's preferred punishment. A community service order was chosen by 41%, prison by 28% and a fine by 13%.
- Within Europe as a whole, the public considered a community service order to be the most appropriate sentence for a recidivist burglar. Those in W.Germany (60%), Switzerland (57%) and France (53%) were particularly in favour of this sanction.
- The percentage of those opting for a prison sentence was highest in Indonesia (67%), the USA (53%) and Poland (42%). In N.Ireland (45%), Scotland (39%), England & Wales (38%), Australia (36%) and Canada (32%) there was also higher than average preference for imprisonment, suggesting a special British tradition of incarcerating burglars.
- Those who had been a victim of burglary (36%) were rather more likely to recommend a sentence of imprisonment than non-victims (27%). Similarly, those in countries with the highest burglary rates were somewhat more likely to recommend imprisonment.
- In all countries, except the USA, those with a higher level of education were more likely to opt for a community service and less likely to choose for a prison sentence.
- A preference for imprisonment was more widespread in countries with relatively high rates of prisoners per 100,000 inhabitants.

Crime prevention

- The percentage of houses protected by a burglar alarm varied widely between the participating countries. An average of 13% of detached, or semi-detached houses were said to have such protection. Burglar alarms were relatively common in England & Wales, Scotland, W.Germany, Belgium and France; they were also relatively common in the three non-European countries.

- Houses with alarms were more often burgled than those without, and countries with high alarm rates had higher burglary risks. This is likely to be because alarms are more often installed in vulnerable houses, perhaps often after a burglary. The present data suggests that burglaries in houses with alarms are less likely to be successful than in houses without alarms.
- Caretakers are common in apartment buildings in the USA (57%), Canada (47%) and Australia (32%), as well as in France, Finland, Norway and Belgium. They are much less common in the Netherlands (12%), Scotland (12%), and Switzerland (3%). There is some suggestion that in countries where caretakers are common, flats with caretakers have lower burglary risks. Generally, the percentage of successful burglaries is lower in flats with caretakers than in those without.
- Leaving lights on when the home is left empty in the evening is done routinely in some countries (eg. the USA, Canada, Norway, and England & Wales) but much less often elsewhere (eg. in France, Spain, Switzerland, and Belgium). The type of dwellings people most often live in may explain this in part.
- Many people ask someone to watch their home when they are away for a day or two. This is somewhat more common in England & Wales and Scotland, and in the three non-European countries. In most countries a sizeable minority does not ask neighbours to watch their home because they expect their neighbours to do that anyway. Houses with such 'natural surveillance' had lower burglary risks than other houses in most countries, either because of surveillance itself, or other associated factors (eg. strong community spirit).

Discussion

This report has offered a great deal of information which those interested in crime will wish to digest. However, not least because of the uniqueness of the results, those examining them may well ask how reliable they are.

As explained in Chapter 1, the survey shares some limitations of crime surveys generally, as regards for example the types of crime that can be measured. These are predominantly 'conventional' crimes against household and personal property, often at the less serious end of the spectrum. Crimes against, and perpetrated by businesses are excluded for one. So too are crimes against younger teenagers (who are far from immune from crime), and those who live outside private households. To encourage wide participation, sample sizes were modest. This affects the scope for detailed analysis, and means that small differences in results will not be statistically reliable. Indeed, all the figures presented are inevitably subject to sampling error, and this should be borne in mind at all times.

Nor can it be known how far the reporting of crime to interviewers was affected by cultural differences in definitions of what constitutes criminal victimization, or by differences in sensitivity about talking about crime. In essence, the survey measures public perceptions of crime as expressed to interviewers, rather than necessarily 'real' experience.

The results are also at country level: jurisdictions within countries may vary in terms of crime risks and attitudes to crime as much as countries themselves differ. Differences in victimization risks according to the size of the place where respondents live is well-known from previous research, and this has been borne out here again.

Telephone ownership

On a more technical front, the use of telephone interviewing is an important issue. There are two aspects of the use of telephone interviewing in the survey that should be considered with regard to potential bias that might have been introduced; firstly, the fact that the proportion of households with telephones in the countries participating in the survey differed; and, second, that there were rather low, and variable response rates. A more detailed assessment of these points can be found in Annex A, but the main conclusions are summarized below.

As the most important difference between owners and non-owners in different countries relates to household income, the possible bias from differential telephone ownership ('non-coverage bias') will centre largely on the relationship between income and experience of crime. Tests of this from the survey data suggest that those with *above-average incomes* (even after controlling for vehicles ownership) face generally *higher* risks of crime. On the face of it, this would suggest two conclusions, although neither appear entirely plausible. First, it might be supposed that victimization risks were somewhat relatively *overestimated* in countries with lower telephone ownership (ie, where a larger proportion of poorer, non-owners have been omitted from the sample); in fact, though, overall risks in the countries to which this would apply were moderately low. Second, the relationship between higher income and higher risk would suggest that the survey has produced rather higher estimates of crime than would have been the case with fuller representation of the population. However, not all other research evidence would be seen endorsing this. Given these inconsistencies, the best conclusion is that non-coverage bias may not be a substantial problem in interpreting relative risks. More importantly, it should be remembered that countries in the survey had generally high telephone coverage, and that the range of non-coverage was not great. The samples taken, therefore, are fairly representative of national populations, and the results are unlikely to be greatly affected by any differences in risks insofar as these are income-related.

Response rates

Refusal to be interviewed is generally held to be the biggest problem as regards bias. One argument about response bias, in particular the most important form of this - refusing to be interviewed - is that victims will be *over-represented* among responders. Victims will be more willing to be interviewed *because* they have been victimized, and this will mean some overestimation of risks in countries where response was poorer. A contrary argument is that with low response rates, people are omitted with whom it is harder to achieve an interview: people who may be more liable to victimization because they are residentially more unstable, if not simply away from home more.

Both positions gain some support from research done in other contexts. Present results do not support either position unequivocally. On the one hand, victimization risks *were* generally higher in countries with the highest non-response, appearing to endorse the idea that victims were overrepresented. However, the relationship was not statistically strong, and intuitively it is not wholly persuasive. For instance, the Netherlands had comparatively low non-response, but comparatively high risks, while Belgium had high non-response, but low risks. It would also seem surprising if risks in the USA were actually lower than has been indicated. On the other hand, there is no strong support either for the contrary argument that low response rates indicate an under-representation of victims, and as a corollary of this that high response rates lead to a relative overestimation of risks. In particular, it again offends intuition to think that risks in Norway, Finland and Switzerland - where response was high - are overestimated in the survey relatively speaking, given that these countries where characterized by noticeably low risks anyway.

In brief, then, the lack of clear evidence on the effects of non-response suggests it may not be an important factor in biassing the results. Possibly, there were counterbalancing effects operating, such that the survey both picked up, and for other reasons lost, a proportion of over-victimized respondents.

Comparison with other indicators

Another way of assessing the present estimates on victimization risks is to see how they compare with other available measures. Three sources of data are relevant: first, the conventional comparative measure of offences recorded by the police ('recorded offences'); second, estimates of crime from independent surveys in individual countries; and, third, the few comparative studies which compare results from individual surveys taking into account methodological differences between them. It can be said in advance that none of these comparisons can be taken very far, though there are positive pointers from all of them.

Police figures

First, how similar is the picture from present results to that from recorded crime? No full correspondence would be expected as the recorded crime measure is itself unstable for comparative purposes. Definitions of offences used by the police will differ between countries. So too will practices on how offences are counted (eg, whether incidents involving several criminal elements are counted as one offence of more). The extent to which offences are recorded at all in a consistent way is also debatable. For instance, 'marginal' criminal incidents, such as minor assaults and attempted burglary, may be handled differently for recording purposes in different countries. Another issue is the degree to which the police are informed of offences by victims: any difference in reporting will undermine the comparability of recorded offences as it will affect the number of potentially recordable offences the police know about.

This said, while there is far from close correspondence between survey results and recorded offences, there is similarity on various fronts. (The similarity relates to respective levels of crime, rather than the amount of crime that would be estimated from the two measures, which will inevitably be different.) Moreover, the two measures are brought more closely in line, as should be the case, when survey figures are adjusted to take account of the extent of crime reported to the police.

For theft of cars - a well-reported and relatively clear-cut offence, there is strong correspondence between how countries compare in terms of recorded offences and present estimates. For burglary, the two measures show fair correspondence for many countries, though less so than with car theft. For robbery, there is weaker correspondence (N.Ireland and W.Germany are particularly out of line), though much more similarity when reported survey crimes are considered. Police and survey measures of assault and sexual crimes are poorly related, though again far more so for reported crime.

These results, then, show that differences in levels of reporting to the police are a major reason why recorded offences are unstable for comparative purposes. If the survey estimates of national crime levels are adjusted for reporting, their ranking is for all five types of crime fairly similar to the one on the basis of police figures. This does much to counter any argument that the results from the present study are strongly biassed for some countries, since a close correspondence with police figures would be unlikely if they were.

Independent surveys

The second comparison is between present estimates and those from victim surveys which individual countries have carried out to estimate the level of reported and unreported crime. The scope for precise matching is limited, since differences in survey design and even small differences in offence classification can seriously affect counts.[1] For present purposes, the most feasible comparison is with surveys with which the Working Group is most familiar.[2] The Group hopes that in due course other participating countries will undertake comparisons with their own surveys, if these are available.

Risks in Switzerland according to present survey are fairly comparable with those found in 1985 and 1986 Swiss surveys, also conducted by telephone (Killias, 1989). Victimization rates in the Netherlands in 1988, as measured by its national survey (Eijken, 1989) also show similar risks for equivalent offence categories, though the present survey produces slightly lower risks for thefts from cars, burglary, and assaults/threats for example.[3] In England & Wales, estimates for 1987 from the British Crime Survey are reasonably well in line, though again rather lower risks emerged from the current survey for thefts from cars, burglary and assaults/threats (authors' calculations).

Broadly, then, taking some account of methodological differences, results from the present survey are not seriously out of line with the independent surveys, though there is a tendency for present estimates to be slightly lower. This is perhaps not unexpected, since other surveys use more extensive methods of 'screening' for victimization. These are likely to prompt a respondent's memory better and uncover more incidents particularly at the less serious end of the range. Results from the present survey show a rather higher proportion of incidents reported to the police, which is consistent with the idea that the survey elicited from respondents a slightly narrower, and more serious, range of offences.

Other comparative studies

The third comparison is how the picture from the present survey accords with that from studies (albeit small in number) which themselves have compared independent surveys, recognising that methodological differences between them need to be taken into account. On balance, the picture is again a fairly reassuring one. For instance, the generally low risks in Switzerland seen in these results are borne out by work by Killias (1989) in

---

1. For example, surveys do not always cover the same age-group. Some ask one person to report on personal crimes on behalf of others in the household - which is likely to underestimate personal risks (eg, Skogan, 1986). The length of the 'recall period' can also differ, with shorter recall periods producing the best memory performance, and highest counts. 'Bounding' procedures are also important, and the singular way in which the NCS of the USA 'bounds' interviews make comparisons with it particularly difficult. The way 'series' offences are counted, and how offences are defined, and classified is also critical (Mayhew, 1987).
2. For these comparisons, some estimates from the present survey have been based on data weighted on a household base when this matches better how results from other surveys have been presented. (See Annex B on weighting.)
3. Though question differences are likely to explain this.

which Swiss victimizations risks are compared with those in the Netherlands, England & Wales, Canada, Australia and the USA. Another feature of the present results is that for many crimes, risks in England & Wales and Scotland are strikingly similar. This was also the result of a comparison of risks in 1981 on the basis of British Crime Survey results (Mayhew and Smith, 1985). Other studies also throw light on a feature of the present results which might be seen as surprising: namely, that while risks for Americans in larger urban areas are generally higher than elsewhere, *average* risks of many crimes across the USA are not especially greater, and even sometimes lower than in other countries. In a comparison of England & Wales, Scotland, the Netherlands, and the USA, Block (1987) found that risks of assaults with force in the USA were similar to those in England & Wales and Scotland, and lower than those in the Netherlands (cf. Hough, 1986). For pickpocketing, Block showed, as does the present survey, that USA risks were lower than in England & Wales and Scotland, and that risks again were highest in the Netherlands. Block's results suggested that USA burglary risks were over twice as high as in England & Wales, Scotland and the Netherlands, though another comparison (Mayhew, 1987) produced results more in line with the present results. In both the present survey and Block's study, thefts from vehicles were highest in the USA, though not markedly so. Thefts of vehicles according to Block and this survey were lowest in the Netherlands, and high in England & Wales; present results give rather higher risks for the USA than Block did.

In summary, then, an attempt has been made to address the reliability of the present results by considering the issues of telephone ownership and response rates, and whether the picture of victimization risks matches other indicators. It cannot be known for certain whether interviewing only those with a telephone at home, and then only some of these, has undermined the comparability of results across country, though the balance of the evidence is that no severe bias has been introduced. The fact that the results of the survey also stand up reasonably well on victimization risks against other indicators adds to their credibility. Other results from the survey, too, are much in line with those from available independent surveys - for example, on who is most afraid of crime, and what sorts of crime are most often reported to the police. In particular, analysis of the main correlates of victimization gives results very much in accord with other findings with respect to age, gender, place of residence, and lifestyle, for instance.

The future

A subsequent report on the study will be published in due course. This will cover results from Japan and report more detailed analysis of specific topics. It will also draw out particular features of the results for each participating country. The Working Group would like to see the survey repeated in as many countries as possible at a later date. On the basis of experience, some modification to the method of data collection seems advisable (eg, the use of CATI preceded by a letter to selected respondents which announces the interview). In the meantime, the questionnaire is available (in many languages) to countries who have not yet conducted crime surveys, and who may wish to use the present results as a benchmark.[4] The questionnaire itself should not be fundamentally changed, to allow comparisons with the present data. Minor changes to some of the secondary questions seem advisable, however.[5] It also seems worth considering extending the questions on precautionary behaviour and crime prevention measures taken.

---

4. Those interested in using the questionnaires should contact Jaap de Waard, Directie Criminaliteitspreventie, Ministerie van Justitie, 2500 EH Den Haag, Holland. The English language version of the questionnaire is at Annex D.
5. The follow-up questions about pickpocketing, sexual assault and assault with force, for instance, would be best asked about all incidents in the last year, rather than the last incident over the five year period only. The question about weapon use would also be better asked about threats as well. Questions about the location of the crime would be useful for sexual incidents and threats/assaults.

7 Summaries in French and German

Resumé

Plan de la recherche

Le présent rapport présente les résultats d'un projet international de recherche dans lequel des études sur l'expérience du crime furent effectuées sur des échantillons représentatifs au niveau national, composés de 1000 à 5000 personnes âgées de 16 ans au moins. Cette étude concernant les expériences face au crime fut effectuée au début 1989. Standardisées quant à la méthode d'échantillonage, d'interview et des questions, ces études furent entreprises dans 14 pays d'Europe et d'outre-mer, c'est-à-dire aux USA, au Canada, en Australie, en France, en Angleterre et au Pays de Galles, en Ecosse, en Irlande du Nord, en Espagne, en République fédérale d'Allemagne, en Suisse, aux Pays-Bas, en Belgique, en Norvège et en Finlande. Trois autres pays (l'Indonésie, la Pologne et le Japon) ont utilisé le même questionnaire, mais avec des techniques d'enquête différentes. Ce rapport se limite en grande partie aux résultats obtenus dans les 14 pays participants, quoique parfois des résultats indonésien ou polonais soient présentés. Les résultats obtenus au Japon ne sont pas encore disponibles.

L'étude a été basée sur des techniques de sondage de victimisation telles qu'elles ont été utilisées, au fil des 20 dernières années, dans un certain nombre de pays. Les résultats de ces sondages nationaux étaient pourtant difficilement comparables au niveau international étant donné les différences dans leur méthodologie. Le travail sur le terrain fut entièrement effectué par interviews téléphoniques informatisées (CATI), à l'exception de l'Irlande du Nord et de l'Espagne (où environ la moitié des interviews se sont déroulées en face-à-face). L'organisation technique de l'étude était effectuée sous la responsabilité d'Inter/View d'Amsterdam, soustraitant dans certains pays avec des compagnies affiliées. L'étude était commandée par les gouvernements des pays participants à l'invitation du groupe de travail constitué par Jan J.M. van Dijk, coordinateur général (Ministère de la Justice, Pays-Bas), Pat Mayhew (Home Office, Grande-Bretagne) et Martin Killias (Université de Lausanne, Suisse).

L'étude apporte une information unique et un aperçu international sur les expériences des gens face au crime et leur réponse à ce phénomène. Mais elle donne surtout une idée de l'étendue de la victimisation criminelle indépendamment de celle véhiculée par les statistiques officielles de police. Ces dernières ne font d'ailleurs qu'énumérer les crimes rapportés et enregistrés par la police et ne sont donc pas propres à des comparaisons internationales. Le présent sondage a recueilli des informations identiques (et donc comparables) dans chaque pays concernant la criminalité et la réponse apportée au problème du crime.

La fréquence des diverses infractions en comparaison internationale

Le but de ce rapport est uniquement de présenter quelques résultats-clés de l'étude en question. Des corrélations plus détaillées et des considérations plus particulières paraîtront dans une prochaine publication. Le risque de victimisation est basé sur le pourcentage des interviewés qui disent avoir été une ou plusieurs fois victime en 1988. Les résultats de Varsovie (Pologne) et de Surabaja (Indonésie) font l'objet d'un paragraphe particulier.

Délits concernant les véhicules

- Le risque de se faire voler sa voiture en 1988 était le plus fort en France (2,3%), aux Etats-Unis (2,1%), en Australie (2,3%) et en Angleterre et au Pays de Galles (1,8%). Ce risque était le moins élevé en Finlande, aux Pays-Bas, en République fédérale d'Allemagne et en Suisse (graphique 1). Cela se modifie peu si l'on ne considère que les ménages qui possèdent une ou plusieurs automobiles, ou si - au delà de l'année 1988 - les cinq dernières années sont examinées (tableau 2, E.2 et E.8).
- Le vol de motos, de motocyclettes et de vélomoteurs est le plus important en Suisse (1,2%), en Espagne (0,8%) et en France (0,6%) (graphique 7). De nouveau, ces taux sont peu influencés par le pourcentage de propriétaires. Durant les cinq dernières années, 17% des propriétaires français et 16% des propriétaires suisses se sont vus subtiliser leurs motocyclettes.
- Le vol de bicyclette est en 1988 de loin le plus important aux Pays-Bas (7,6%). Des taux assez élevés se rencontrent aussi pour la République fédérale d'Allemagne (3,3%), le Canada (3,4%), les Etats-Unis (3,1%), la Finlande (3,1%) et la Suisse (3,2%) (graphique 8). Dans tous ces pays il est assez commun de posséder une bicyclette, ceci tout particulièrement aux Pays-Bas.
- Ces résultats montrent bien que l'un des facteurs déterminants du nombre de vols de véhicules est la disponibilité des cibles à voler (graphiques 28 et 29). Là où il y a beaucoup de voitures ou bicyclettes, le risque individuel de se faire voler sa voiture est plus important pour les propriétaires, le nombre de cibles étant plus importante. C'est ainsi que si l' 'offre' augmente, il en ira en plus avec la 'demande'. Les vols de bicyclettes surtout (ou le risque de vol pour chaque bicyclette) augmentent en relation avec la quantité de tels véhicles sur le marché.

- Là où le vol de voitures est faible, celui des bicyclette est important (graphique 30). Il semble donc que les délinquants qui volent dans le but de pouvoir se déplacer temporairement se contentent d'une bicyclette dès le moment où il y en a suffisamment.
- En 1988, le vol dans les voitures (bagages, autoradio, rétroviseurs, etc.) fut le plus important en Espagne (9,9%), aux Etats-Unis (9,3%) et au Canada (7,2%). Pour la Suisse, la Finlande, la Norvège et la Belgique ce risque était assez faible (graphique 3).
- Le risque d'actes de vandalisme dirigés contre une voiture était le plus important au Canada (9,8%), en République fédérale d'Allemagne (8,7%), aux Etats-Unis (8,9%) et en Australie (8,7%). Par contre, les risques les plus faibles furent enregistrés en Finlande, en Suisse, en Norvège et en Irlande du Nord (graphique 5, tableau 2).
- Le taux élevé de risque de vol de voiture et de vandalisme contre les véhicules relevé aux Etats-Unis et au Canada peut être en partie expliqué par le pourcentage assez élevé de propriétaires dans ces pays.

Vol par effraction

- En 1988, les voleurs se sont le plus souvent introduits dans les maisons en Australie (4,4%), aux Etats-Unis (3,8%) et au Canada (3,0%). En Europe, le risque le plus élevé fut trouvé en France (2,4%), aux Pays-Bas (2,4%) et en Belgique (2,3%). La Norvège, la Finlande et la Suisse présentent les plus faibles taux de risque (graphique 10). Les tentatives de vol par effraction connaissent une répartition internationale analogue (graphique 12).

Brigandage

- En 1988, le vol commis avec violence ou menace était le plus fréquent en Espagne (2,8% des personnes interrogées) et aux Etats-Unis (1,9%). Pour le reste, le taux de brigandage en Europe se situait au-dessous de 1% (graphique 13). En Espagne, dans 40% des cas, le délinquant avait recours à un couteau (contre 20% en moyenne de tous les pays). Aux Etats-Unis, 28% des délinquants se servaient d'un pistolet, contre 8% en moyenne. L'utilisation plus fréquente d'armes de poing lors de brigandages aux Etats-Unis est certainement à mettre en relation avec la pénétration plus importante de ces armes dans la population américaine. Selon les résultats de l'enquête ci-dessus, 29% des ménages américains possèdent une telle arme à feu, contre 6% en moyenne. En outre, on trouve relativement fréquemment des armes de poing en Belgique et en Allemagne (7% des ménages), en France (6%) ainsi qu'en Suisse (14%), mais dans ce dernier pays plus de la moitié sont des armes de service (graphique 48).

Vol simple et vol à la tire

- En 1988, les autres vols (à savoir ceux où aucune violence n'a été exercée) ont été rapportés relativement fréquemment par nos répondants Canadiens (5,4%), Espagnols (5,0%) et Australiens (5,0%); des taux élevés ont également été enregistrés pour les 5 dernières années en Suisse, en Belgique et en Australie, bien que de manière générale la distribution internationale est plus régulière ici que pour d'autres délits (graphique 15). Si l'on ne considère que les vols à la tire, les taux européens (et particulièrement ceux de l'Espagne, de la France, de la Hollande et de la Suisse) dépassent largement ceux des autres continents en 1988 (graphique 16). Il est intéressant de constater la victimisation plus importante des femmes concernant les vols à la tire; cela est vraisemblablement à mettre en relation avec leur utilisation plus fréquente de sacs à main.
- Lors de la comparaison internationale des victimisations contre la personne, et plus particulièrement des vols, il est indispensable de prendre en considération le fait que bon nombre de personnes interrogées ont été victimes d'un délit lors de voyages à l'étranger. En Finlande, en Belgique et en Allemagne fédérale les taux correspondants se situaient entre 8% et 9% (en moyenne de tous les pays: 4%); en Suisse il était de 16% (21% pour les vols).

Violences sexuelles

- Seules les femmes ont été interrogées au sujet des attaques à caractère sexuel. Ce sont les femmes des trois pays non-europeéens qui ont rapporté ce délit le plus souvent: 7,3% en Australie, 4,5% aux USA et 4% au Canada. En Europe, le risque le plus élevé a été relevé en République fédérale d'Allemagne, aux Pays-Bas et en Espagne. On doit cependant interpêter ces résultats de manière prudente, puisque les femmes peuvent être plus ou moins ouvertes à cette question, suivant les différentes cultures. A cela s'ajoute que la question d'entrée (No. 124) était très large et n'enregistrait de ce fait pas seulement des comportements délictueux. C'est ainsi que grâce à la question complémentaire (No. 235), on put relever, parmi les incidents signalés, 3% de viols consommés, 9% de tentatives de viols et 17% d'agressions à caractère sexuel, contre 69% d'incidents que les personnes intérrogées qualifiaient d'"offensant' (graphiques 18 et 19).
- Les attaques à caractère sexuel punissables (viols, tentatives de viol et autres agressions à caractère sexuel) sont le plus élevé aux USA (2,3% de femmes ayent indiqué un tel délit), au Canada (1,7%), en Australie (1,6%), et en Allemagne fédérale (1,5%).

Coups et blessures et menaces

- Les coups et blessures et les menaces paraissent avoir une répartition internationale identique à celle des attaques à caractère sexuel contre les femmes. En 1988, ces incidents étaient les plus fréquents dans les trois pays non-européens, suivis de la République fédérale d'Allemagne, de l'Espagne, des Pays-Bas et de la Norvège (graphique 21). Si l'on ne considère que les cas où violence a été faite à la victime, excluant donc les cas de simple menace, le risque le plus élevé se situe également aux Etats-Unis et en Australie; en Europe, c'est en Finlande, en Hollande et en Allemagne (graphique 22) que le risque est le plus élevé.

Appréciation globale

- Pour l'année 1988, les taux de victimisation, tous crimes confondus, furent les plus importants aux Etats-Unis (29%), au Canada (28%) et en Australie (28%). En Europe, les taux les plus importants furent enregistrés aux Pays-Bas (27%), suivis de l'Espagne (25%) et de la République fédérale d'Allemagne (22%). Les taux les plus faibles furent relevés en Irlande du Nord (15%), en Finlande (16%), en Norvège (17%) et en Suisse (16%) (graphique 25). La moitié environ des délits enregistrés ont été perpétrés à proximité du domicile de la victime, un tiers ailleurs dans la ville ou la localité de domicile, et grosso modo une infraction sur dix a eu lieu quelque part ailleurs dans le pays. Dans plusieurs pays, un nombre non négligeable de délits eurent lieu à l'étranger (cf. ci-dessus).
- La caractéristique des pays à faible criminalité est d'avoir un taux d'urbanisation très peu élevé. De ce fait, une bonne partie des personnes interrogées vit dans des petits villages et très peu d'entre elles résident dans des villes de plus de 100.000 habitants (graphique 27).
- Le risque de victimisation à Varsovie (Pologne) correspond approximativement à celui des grandes villes de l'Europe de l'Ouest. A Surabaja (Indonésie), ce taux est relativement bas, particulièrement pour le vols de voiture et les coups et blessures (tableau 1).
- Les taux de victimisation dans les villes de plus de 100.000 habitants sont généralements plus élevés aux USA que partout ailleurs, bien qu'il y ait des exceptions pour certains délits. Les taux des villes canadiennes et européenne sont très semblables. Les taux dans villes australiennes sont assez variables selon le délit pris en compte, main géneralement ils se situent en dessous de eux des villes américaines et canadiennes.

Comparaison entre notre enquête et les statistiques de police

- Lors d'une comparaison entre les taux de délits dénoncés dans les différents pays, et les taux correspondants de la statistique criminelle d'INTERPOL, nous avons relevé des corrélations assez fortes. La

115

meilleure correspondance est constatée pour les vols de voitures, délit particulièrement souvent dénoncé. Pour ce qui est du brigandage, des coups et blessures et des violences sexuelles, on constate également une correspondance plus élevée lorsque l'on ne considère que les délits que nos victimes prétendent avoir dénoncé à la police.

- Etant donné que les résultats de cette étude ne dépendent aucunement de la dénonciation, ni de la pratique d'enregistrement de la part de la police, ils donnent probablement une image plus représentative de la distribution internationale de la criminalité que les statistiques de police.

Les délits et leurs victimes

Répartition sociale du risque de victimisation

- Dans la majeure partie des infractions, les hommes courent un plus grand risque de victimisation que les femmes; de même le risque est plus élevé chez les jeunes que chez les rentiers. De plus, les habitants des grandes villes sont plus fréquemment victimes pour ce qui concerne les infractions considérées ici. Il apparaît que les sorties nocturnes plus fréquentes des jeunes hommes et filles dans les villes augmentent leur risque de victimisation (tableaux 4 et 5).
- Dans les pays où un grand nombre de femmes exercent une activité professionelle, le risque de victimisation tend à s'équilibrer pour les deux sexes. Dans les pays avec un faible taux de femmes actives par contre (Pays-Bas, Irlande, Suisse), le risque de subir une infraction est nettement plus faible pour les femmes que pour les hommes.
- En ce qui concerne les vols, ce sont les classes de revenus les plus élevées qui sont le plus souvent frappées.

Reportabilité des infractions

- Pour tous les crimes considérés dans le sondage, une moyenne de 50% a été dénoncée à la police en 1988. Le pourcentage de crimes rapportés à la police varie selon le type de délit. Certains délits contre la propriété ont un taux de reportabilité relativement élevé: par exemple le vol de voiture (93%), le cambriolage (77%) et le vol de vélo (60%). Le brigandage a un taux de reportabilité moins élevé (49%), comme cela est également le cas pour les autres types de vol (41%), les attaques corporelles (31%) et le vandalisme contre les voitures (39%). Les attaques sexuelles sont les infractions les moins souvent dénoncées (12%); il faut cependant garder à l'esprit que les victimes de 69% des incidents signalés ne les qualifiaient que d'actes 'offensants', c'est-à-dire à la limite de la punissabilité. Les violences sexuelles graves (avec 24%) et plus particulièrement les viols (avec 48%) sont plus souvent rapportés à la police. (Sur la fréquence de la reportabilité selon les délits et les pays pris en compte, voir les graphiques 2, 4, 6, 9, 11, 14, 17, 20, 23 et table E.4.)

116

- Dans l'ensemble, les pourcentages de reportabilité ont été relativement faibles en Indonésie (18%), en Espagne (34%), en Pologne (41%), en Norvège (43%) et en Finlande (45%) (graphique 33). Les personnes aux revenus les plus modestes ont moins souvent dénoncé les infractions dont elle avaient été victimes (38%) que les autres (51%).
- Les principales raisons données par les victimes (de tous les pays considérés) pour ne pas rapporter le délit à la police ont été que l'infraction n'était: "pas assez grave" (40%), que "la police ne pouvait rien faire" (19%), ou que "la police ne ferait rien" (10%). La fréquence de ces réponses était en général uniforme à travers tous les pays considérés. Il existe cependant également un lien entre le fait de posséder une assurance contre le cambriolage (et la diffusion de telles assurances dans les divers pays) et la reportabilité, les assurés dénoncent en effet plus souvent que les autres (87% contre 65%).
- Quand elles ont dénoncé une infraction à la police, la plupart des victimes ont été satisfaites de la manière dont elles ont été traitées (66%). Un niveau relativement faible de satisfaction a été exprimé par les victimes en Pologne (20%), en Norvège (33%), en Espagne (47%), en France (49%), et en Belgique (53%) (graphique 34). Les principales raisons pour lesquelles les victimes n'étaient pas satisfaites ont été que "la police n'en a pas fait assez" (41%), ou "qu'elle n'était pas intéressée" (41%).

Attitude face à la police

- Les deux tiers de la population interrogée ont estimé que la police avait fait du bon travail de prévention du crime dans leur zone d'habitation. On trouve les taux de satisfaction les plus élevés au Canada (89%), aux USA (81%), à Surabaja (76%) et en Australie (73%).
- Le mécontentement vis-à-vis de la police fut le plus élevé en Pologne (69%); des critiques à l'égard de la police ont également été exprimées en Espagne (29%), en République fédérale d'Allemagne (24%) et en Belgique (22%) (grafique 35).
- Cependant, il semble qu'il n'y ait aucun lien à établir avec les taux de criminalité dans les divers pays. Les victimes d'infractions (en 1988) étaient toutefois moins contentes de la police que ne l'étaient les non-victimes (25 contre 16%).

Assistance aux victimes

- Seuls 3,8% des victimes d'infractions qui ont été denoncées à la police ont reçu (tous les pays pris en compte) une aide quelconque de la part d'une agence spécialisée pour donner des informations ou une aide matérielle et morale aux victimes de crimes. Ce pourcentage fut un peu plus élevé aux USA (10%), au Canada (5,5%), en Belgique (6,4%), en Finlande (4,4%) et en Angleterre et au Pays de Galles (4,0%) (graphique

36). Les pourcentages de ceux qui ont reçu une aide spécialisée furent plus élevés parmi des victimes d'une agression à caractère sexuel (15,1%), d'une vol commis avec violence ou menace (8,6%), d'un cambriolage (7,7%), et de coups et blessures (7,3%). Les femmes (4,1%) et les personnes aux revenus modestes (5,8%) ont également bénéficié plus souvent d'une telle aide.

- La plus grande partie des victimes a déclaré que les services d'une telle organisation leur auraient été utils (35%), ceci tout particulièrement en Indonésie et en Pologne (graphique 37).
- Le souhait d'une telle aide se fait particulièrement ressentir chez les victimes d'une agression à caractère sexuel. Le sexe et l'âge n'ont d'ailleurs aucune influence dans ce domaine.
- Dans tous les pays, le nombre de ceux qui aspirent à une telle aide est bien plus élevé que le nombre de ceux qui en ont effectivement profité.

Réaction face à la criminalité

La peur du crime

- Les répondants furent interrogés, dans le cadre de cette recherche, sur les précautions prises lors de leur sortie nocturne (sortie uniquement accompagnée/éviter certains endroits pour empêcher une infraction) et sur la probabilité d'être victime d'un cambriolage au cours des 12 mois à venir. Les résultats montrent que l'appréciation subjective du risque de cambriolage correspond à la fréquence réelle des cambriolages dans le pays considéré (graphique 40).
- Par contre, la fréquence des précautions face aux délits contre la personne ne concorde pas avec le risque de tels délits, même s'il y a des différences sur le plan international (graphique 38). Celles-ci sont particulièrement répendues en Allemagne, en Angleterre et au Pays de Galles, aux USA ainsi qu'à Varsovie et à Surabaja. Il apparaît dans l'ensemble que les femmes prennent plus souvent de telles mesures que les hommes. Il en va de même pour les victimes de délits contre la personne (plus particulièrement les femmes) si on les compare aux non-victimes.

Punitivité

- On a demandé à tous les répondants de cette enquête, quelle serait la meilleure sanction pour un cambrioleur récidiviste de 21 ans qui vient de dérober un appareil TV couleur. Le service à la communauté fut choisi par 41% des personnes intérrogées, la prison par 28% et l'amende par 13% (résultats donnés pour tous les pays pris en compte). Le pourcentage de ceux qui ont choisi une peine ferme fut supérieur à la moyenne en Indonésie, aux USA, en Pologne, en Irlande du Nord, en Ecosse, en Angleterre et au Pays de Galles, en Australie et au Canada, tandis que le service à la communauté (Community Service Order) semble plus

118

populaire en République fédérale d'Allemagne (60%), en Suisse (57%) et en France (53%) (tableau 9).
- En comparant pour chaque pays le nombre de personnes interrogées qui se sont prononcées en faveur d'une peine ferme avec le taux de prisonniers (sur 100.000 habitants) du pays respectif, il apparaît dans le public une préference en faveur de l'emprisonnement dans les pays avec un taux relativement élevé de délinquants incarcérés (graphique 41). Les adeptes de l'emprisonnement sont plus nombreux parmi les victimes d'un cambriolage ainsi que dans les pays à haut taux de cambriolages.

Mesures matérielles de précautions

- Des questions ont été posées sur les mesures éventuellement prises pour éviter un cambriolage, telles que la pose d'une alarme, l'engagement d'un gardien d'immeuble (dans les immeubles locatifs) et sur l'habitude de laisser les lumières allumées ou d'avertir les voisins lors des absences.
- En ce qui concerne les systèmes d'alarme, il apparaît un faible lien avec le risque de cambriolage dans les divers pays considérés (graphique 44) en ce sens qu'un tel système est plus répandu dans les pays connaissant un grand risque de cambriolage. Probablement de tels systèmes sont installés quand le risque de cambriolage - par exemple à la suite d'une expérience analogue - semble plus élevé. Le pourcentage de maisons protégées par un sytème de sécurité contre les cambriolages varie fortement entre les pays participants.
- Les alarmes contre les cambriolages sont relativement fréquentes en Angleterre et au Pays de Galles, en Ecosse, en Belgique, en Allemagne, ainsi qu'aux USA, au Canada et en Australie (graphique 43). Les maisons avec alarme sont plus souvent cambriolées que celles sans alarme. Ceci provient certainement du fait que les alarmes sont plus souvent installées dans des maisons vulnérables et après un cambriolage. Elles semblent d'ailleurs réduire quelque peu le risque d'un cambriolage réussi.
- Le nombre de concierges (gardiens d'immeuble) dans les maisons locatives varie fortement d'un pays à l'autre (graphique 42) probablement pour des raisons (y compris la tradition) qui n'ont rien à voir avec le risque de cambriolage; pourtant de nos jours ils sont également considérés comme moyen de protection. Les gardiens sont fréquents dans les immeubles locatifs aux USA (57% des personnes interrogées vivant dans de tels immeubles), au Canada (47%) et en Australie (32%), ainsi qu'en France, en Finlande, en Norvège et en Belgique. Ils sont moins fréquents aux Pays-Bas (12%), en Ecosse (12%) et en Suisse (3%). En France, en Belgique et au Canada, les maisons protégées par un concierge sont cambrioleés moins souvent que les autres.
- Laisser les lumières allumées le soir quand la maison reste vide est une pratique courante dans divers pays (par exemple aux USA, en Angleterre et au Pays de Galles et en Norvège), mais beaucoup plus rare ailleurs (par exemple en Espagne, en France, en Suisse et en Finlande). Les types

d'habitation dans lesquelles les gens résident expliquent en partie ces différences (graphique 45).

- Un nombre quelque peu plus élevé d'interrogés du Royaume-Uni et des trois pays non-européens demandent à quelqu'un de s'occuper de sa maison lors d'absences prolongées (graphique 46). Dans un grand nombre de pays, une bonne partie de la population s'abstient de demander aux voisins de s'occuper de leur appartement en pensant que ceux-ci le font d'office. Les maisons avec une telle 'surveillance naturelle' sont moins souvent cambriolées que les autres. Cela souligne l'importance de la 'surveillance naturelle' pour la prévention du cambriolage.

Remarques finales

Bien que ces résultats soient uniques et donnent lieu à de nombreuses réflexions, certaines limites du sondage international doivent être mises en évidence. Comme cela à été expliqué au chapitre 1, le sondage connait les limites des sondages de victimisation en général, par exemple les erreurs d'échantillonage et le choix des infractions - principalement des crimes 'conventionnels' et peu graves. De plus, pour encourager une large participation des pays et diminuer les frais, la taille de l'échantillon a été fixée à un niveau assez modeste, ce qui affecte clairement la force des résultats et limite les possibilités d'en tirer des analyses plus fines.

Une autre source d'imprécision provient du fait que la pénétration du téléphone varie d'un pays à l'autre. Cela peut influencer les résultats dans la mesure où les non-possesseurs de téléphone peuvent avoir des expériences et des attitudes différentes face au crime. Il est impossible de savoir dans quelle mesure la disponibilité des personnes interrogées, auxquelles les auteurs de l'interview demandaient de signaler les crimes dont elles avaient été les victimes, a été affectée par des différences culturelles (sur la définition des infractions retenues), ou des différences de sensibilité et de tempérament. Pour l'essentiel, le sondage mesure la perception du public plutôt qu'il ne reflète nécessairement une expérience 'réelle'. Ensuite, le sondage de victimisation renseigne plus sur l'expérience subjective de la criminalité que sur les faits réels. Finalement, les résultats sont à l'échelon du pays: les juridictions internes peuvent varier en termes de risque de criminalité et même d'attitude face au crime tout autant que les pays eux-mêmes diffèrent entre eux.

Il n'est pas facile de savoir dans quelle mesure les facteurs méthodologiques ont influencé les résultats observés, mais le groupe de travail estime qu'il n'y a pas eu de graves distorsions. Plusieurs résultats sont en accord avec les connaissances établies, par exemple au sujet des facteurs de risques de victimisation. D'autres confirment les connaissances criminologiques sur le profil du crime dans différents pays.

Un rapport subséquent sur l'étude comportant les résultats d'analyses plus approfondies sera publié dans un proche avenir. Le groupe de travail estime qu'il serait utile de répéter le sondage dans le plus grand nombre de pays possible à une date ultérieure. Sur la base de cette expérience, quelques petites modifications sur la méthode de récolte des données semblent judicieuses (par exemple: des échantillons plus étendus, et l'utilisation du système CATI précédé d'une lettre aux répondants sélectionnés qui leur annonce l'interview). En attendant, le questionnaire est à la disposition des pays qui n'ont pas encore fait l'expérience d'un sondage de victimisation et qui désirent utiliser les présents résultats comme point de référence.[1]

---

1. Jaap de Waard, Directie Criminaliteitspreventie, Ministerie van Justitie, 2500 EH Den Haag, Holland.

Zusammenfassung

Untersuchungsanlage

Der vorliegende Bericht enthält die Ergebnisse eines internationalen Forschungsprojekt, in dessen Rahmen repräsentative nationale Bevölkerungsstichproben (ab 16 Jahren) in verschiedenen Ländern anfangs 1989 über ihre Erfahrungen mit Kriminalität befragt wurden. Diese Befragung fand in vierzehn Ländern in und außerhalb Europas nach einer einheitlichen Methodik (hinsichtlich Auswahlverfahren, Befragungsmethode und Fragebogen) statt, nämlich in den Vereinigten Staaten von Amerika, in Kanada, Australien, Frankreich, England und Wales, Schottland, Nordirland, Spanien, in der Bundesrepublik Deutschland, der Schweiz, den Niederlanden, Belgien, Norwegen und Finnland; in weiteren drei Ländern (Polen, Japan und Indonesien) fanden Befragungen mittels desselben Fragebogens, aber anderen Befragungstechniken statt. Im vorliegenden Bericht werden vor allem die Ergebnisse aus den hauptsächlichen vierzehn Teilnehmerstaaten dargestellt; daneben werden auch einzelne Aspekte der indonesischen und der polnischen Untersuchungen aufgegriffen. Die Ergebnisse aus Japan liegen noch nicht vor.

Die Befragung beruhte auf erprobten Techniken der Kriminalitätsmessung anhand von Befragungen, wie sie in verschiedenen Ländern bereits früher durchgeführt worden waren, wobei es sich allerdings als kaum möglich erwies, angesichts der unterschiedlichen Erhebungsmethoden und Auswertungsverfahren die Ergebnisse der früheren Untersuchungen miteinander international zu vergleichen. Bei der vorliegenden Untersuchung wurde fast überall auf die Methode der computergestützten Telefonbefragung zurückgegriffen (CATI), mit Ausnahme in Nordirland und in Spanien (wo rund die Hälfte der Interviews persönlich durchgeführt wurden). Die technische Leitung der Untersuchung lag in den Händen von Inter/View in Amsterdam, die zur Durchführung der Untersuchungen in den einzelnen Ländern verschiedene Partnerfirmen beizog. In Auftrag gegeben wurden die Untersuchung von den Regierungen der teilnehmenden Länder, wobei die Initiative dazu von einer Arbeitsgruppe ausging, welcher Dr. Jan J.M. van Dijk (vom Justizministerium der Niederlande) als Projektkoordinator, Frau Dr. Pat Mayhew (vom britischen Home Office) und Prof. Martin Killias (Universität Lausanne, Schweiz) angehörten.

Die vorliegende Untersuchung gewährt einen - beim heutigen Erkentnisstand - einzigartigen internationalen Ueberblick über die Erfahrungen der Menschen in verschiedenen Ländern mit Kriminalität und ihre Reaktion hierauf. Vor allem verschafft sie eine - von der Kriminalstatistik unabhängige - Vorstellung über das Ausmaß derjenigen Verbrechen in den einzelnen Ländern, die sich gegen den Einzelnen als Opfer richten. Dazu ist die Kriminalstatistik nicht in der Lage, da sie nur diejenigen Verbrechen verzeichnet, die der Polizei angezeigt und von ihr aufgenommen worden sind. Sei eignen sich zudem nicht für internationale Quervergleiche, wie sich bei früheren Bemühungen dieser Art gezeigt hat.

Die Häufigkeit einzelner Straftaten im internationalen Vergleich

Der vorliegende Bericht enthält lediglich eine Darstellung der hauptsächlichen Ergebnisse. Eine ausführliche Würdigung der beobachteten Zusammenhänge und die Darstellung weiterer Einzelheiten sind auf einen späteren Zeitpunkt vorgesehen. Soweit nicht anders angegeben, beziehen sich die im folgenden wiedergegebenen Opferraten auf die Anzahl der Befragten (in Prozent), die ihren Antworten während des Interviews zufolge im Jahre 1988 ein- oder mehrmals Opfer einer Straftat geworden sind. Auf die Ergebnisse aus Warschau (Polen) und Surabaja (Indonesien) wird in einem besonderen Abschnitt eingegangen.

Fahrzeugdiebstähle und dgl.

- Am vergleichsweise höchsten war 1988 das Risiko eines Autodiebstahls in Frankreich (2.3%), in den Vereinigten Staaten (2.1%), in Australien (2.3%) sowie in England und Wales (1.8%), am geringsten in Finnland, in den Niederlanden, in der Bundesrepublik Deutschland und in der Schweiz (Graphik 1). Hieran ändert sich wenig, wenn nur Haushalte berücksichtigt werden, die über wenigstens ein Automobil verfügen, oder wenn - über das Jahr 1988 hinaus - die letzten fünf Jahre insgesamt betrachtet werden (Tabelle 2, E.2 und E.8).
- Am häufigsten waren 1988 die Diebstähle von Motorrädern/Motorfahrrädern und dgl. in der Schweiz (1.2%), Spanien (0.8%) und Frankreich (0.6%) (Graphik 7). In diesen Ländern war allerdings auch die Zahl der Haushalte mit derartigen Fahrzeugen am größten. Wird allein auf Haushalte mit Motorrädern/Motorfahrrädern und dgl. und auf die letzten fünf Jahre abgestellt, so verringern sich die Unterschiede, verschwinden aber nicht; die entsprechenden Raten betragen diesfalls 17% für Frankreich und 16% für die Schweiz (Tabelle 2 und E.8).
- Fahrraddiebstähle waren 1988 am weitaus häufigsten in den Niederlanden (7.6%), wo auch die meisten Fahrräder gehalten werden, gefolgt von Deutschland (3.3%), Kanada (3.4%), den Vereinigten Staaten (3.1%), Finnland (3.1%) und der Schweiz (3.2%) (Graphik 8, Tabelle 2).
- Insgesamt legen diese Ergebnisse den Schluß nahe, daß die Zahl der Fahrzeugdiebstähle von der Häufigkeit der entsprechenden Art von Fahrzeugen abhängt (Graphik 28 und 29). Dabei nimmt das relative Risiko der Fahrzeughalter mit der Häufigkeit der entsprechenden Fahrzeugart potentiell zu: mit zunehmendem "Angebot" steigt somit auch die "Nachfrage". Vor allem Fahrraddiebstähle (bzw. das Diebstahlsrisiko pro Fahrrad) nehmen mit steigender Fahrraddichte Rate zu.
- Bemerkenswert ist auch, daß Autodiebstähle dort häufiger vorkommen, wo seltener Fahrräder gestohlen werden (Graphik 30). Möglicherweise

begnügen sich viele Fahrzeugdiebe, die nach einer sofortigen Transportmöglichkeit Ausschau halten, mit einem Fahrrad, sofern diese in genügender Zahl vorkommen.

- Diebstähle aus Automobilen (Gepäck, Radio, Autobestandteile usw.) kamen 1988 am häufigsten vor in Spanien (9.9%), in den Vereinigten Staaten (9.3%) und in Kanada (7.2%), am seltensten in der Schweiz, in Norwegen, Finnland und Belgien (Graphik 3, Tabelle 2). Die mutwillige Beschädigung von Automobilen wurde am häufigsten von den Befragten in Kanada (9.8%) berichtet, gefolgt von denjenigen in Deutschland (8.7%), in Australien (8.7%) und in den Vereinigten Staaten (8.9%). Am seltensten wurden diese Formen von Sachbeschädigung in Finnland, Norwegen, Nordirland und in der Schweiz festgestellt (Graphik 5, Tabelle 2).
- Die hohen diesbezüglichen Opferraten in Kanada und in den Vereinigten Staaten dürften mit der ausgeprägten Motorisierung in diesen Ländern zusammenhängen.

Einbruchdiebstähle

- Wohnungseinbrüche kamen 1988 am häufigsten vor in Australien (4.4%), in den Vereinigten Staaten (3.8%) und in Kanada (3.0%). Innerhalb Europas verzeichneten Frankreich, die Niederlande und Belgien ebenfalls relativ hohe Raten, wogegen das entsprechende Risiko in Norwegen, Finnland und der Schweiz relativ gering ist (Graphik 10). Versuchte Wohnungseinbrüche weisen eine ähnliche internationale Verteilung auf (Graphik 12).

Raub

- Am meisten Opfer von Raub (d.h. Diebstähle unter Anwendung oder Androhung von Gewalt) wurden in Spanien (2.8% der Befragten) und in den Vereinigten Staaten (1.9%) festgestellt. Innerhalb Europas lag die Rate im übrigen unter 1% (Graphik 13).
- Als Tatwaffe wurde in Spanien in 40% der Fälle ein Messer verwendet (gegenüber 20% im Durchschnitt aller Länder), während in den Vereinigten Staaten 28 % der Täter eine Pistole benutzten (gegenüber 8% im Durchschnitt aller Länder).
- Die häufigere Verwendung von Handfeuerwaffen bei Raub in den Vereinigten Staaten dürfte mit der größeren Verbreitung derartiger Waffen in der amerikanischen Bevölkerung zusammenhängen. Den Ergebnissen der vorliegenden Untersuchung zufolge besitzen 29% der amerikanischen Haushalte eine Handfeuerwaffe, gegenüber 6% im Durchschnitt der übrigen Länder. Relativ verbreitet sind Handfeuerwaffen im übrigen in Belgien und in Deutschland (mit je 7%), in Frankreich (6%) sowie vor allem in der Schweiz (14%), wobei im letzteren Fall allerdings gut die Hälfte Armeepistolen sind (Graphik 48).

Einfache und Taschendiebstähle

- Andere Diebstähle (d.h. solche, die ohne Gewalt verübt wurden) wurden 1988 relativ häufig von den Befragten in Kanada (5.4%), Spanien (5.0%) und Australien (5.0%) berichtet; ebenfalls relativ hoch lag die Rate für die zurückliegenden fünf Jahre in der Schweiz, in Belgien und in Australien, wobei generell die internationale Verteilung gleichmäßiger ist als bei anderen Delikten (Graphik 15).
- Betrachtet man allein die Taschendiebstähle, so lag die Rate in Europa (und besonders in Spanien, Frankreich, in den Niederlanden und in der Schweiz im Jahre 1988 deutlich höher als in den überseeischen Ländern (Graphik 16). Interessant ist das höhere Opferrisiko der Frauen bei Taschendiebstählen, das wohl mit der häufigeren Verwendung von Handtaschen und dgl. zusammenhängen dürfte.
- Bei der Würdigung der internationalen Verteilung der Straftaten gegen die Person im allgemeinen und der Diebstähle im besonderen wird man berücksichtigen müssen, daß die Befragten in einzelnen Ländern einen erheblichen Teil davon bei Auslandreisen erfahren. Bei den Befragten in Finnland, in Belgien und in der Bundesrepublik Deutschland lag der entsprechende Anteil (alle Delikte) bei 8-9% (bei einem Durchschnitt aller Länder von 4%); bei den Schweizern lag er gar bei 16% (und 21% bei den Diebstählen).

Sexuelle Angriffe

- Ueber sexuell motivierte Angriffe wurden ausschließlich Frauen befragt. Am häufigsten wurden derartige Erlebnisse in den drei überseeischen Ländern berichtet (Australien, 7.3%, USA (4.5%), Kanada, 4%). Innerhalb Europas lag die entsprechende Rate am höchsten in Deutschland, Spanien und in den Niederlanden. Dabei wird man allerdings berücksichtigen müssen, daß die Bereitschaft der Befragten, über derartige Vorkommnisse im Rahmen eines Interviews zu berichten, von kulturellen Faktoren mitbestimmt werden dürfte und daher von Land zu Land möglicherweise variiert.
- Dazu kommt, daß die entsprechende Eingangsfrage (Nr. 124) bewußt relativ weit gefaßt war und daher auch nicht unbedingt strafbare Verhaltensweisen erfaßt wurden. So wurden bei der entsprechenden Zusatzfrage (Nr. 235) 3% der Vorfälle als vollendet, 9% als versuchte Vergewaltigung und 17% als gewaltsamer sexueller Angriff bezeichnet - gegenüber 69%, die die Opfer als 'freche Unanständigkeit' einstuften (Graphik 18 und 19).
- Strafbare sexuelle Angriffe (Vergewaltigung einschliesslich Versuche und gewaltsame sexuelle Angriffe) wurden am häufigsten von den befragten Frauen in den USA (2.3%), in Kanada (1.7%), in Australien (1.6%) und in der Bundesrepublik Deutschland (1.5%) berichtet.

Tätliche Angriffe und Drohung

- Tätliche Angriffe und Drohung mit Gewalt scheinen eine ähnliche internationale Verteilung aufzuweisen wie sexuelle Angriffe gegen Frauen. Am häufigsten wurden derartige Vorkommnisse von den Befragten in den drei überseeischen Ländern berichtet, gefolgt von den Befragten in Deutschland, Spanien, den Niederlanden und in Norwegen (Graphik 21).
- Werden allein diejenigen Fälle berücksichtigt, in denen es zu Gewaltanwendung gegen das Opfer (und nicht allein zur Drohung damit) gekommen ist, so lag das Risiko wiederum am höchsten in den Vereinigten Staaten und in Australien; innerhalb Europas werden derartige Erlebnisse von den Befragten in Finnland, in den Niederlanden und in Deutschland ebenfalls relativ häufig berichtet (Graphik 22).

Gesamtbelastung

- Werden alle erhobenen Delikte zusammen berücksichtigt, so lag 1988 das Opferrisiko am höchsten in den Vereinigten Staaten (mit 29%), in Kanada und Australien (mit je 28%). In Europa stehen die Niederlande (mit 27%) an der Spitze, gefolgt von Spanien (25%) und Deutschland (22%). Am geringsten ist das Opferrisiko in bezug auf die vorliegend erhobenen Straftaten in Nordirland (15%), Finnland, Norwegen und in der Schweiz (mit je 16%) (Graphik 25).
- Rund die Hälfte der Straftaten wurden in der Nähe der Wohnung des Opfers verübt, rund ein Drittel anderswo am Wohnort oder in dessen Umgebung, und rund 10% anderswo im betreffenden Land. In verschiedenen Ländern widerfuhr ein nicht unerheblicher Anteil der Straftaten den Befragten im Ausland (siehe oben).
- Länder mit geringem Opferrisiko zeichnen sich durch einen geringen Grad an Urbanisierung aus, d.h. ein erheblicher Teil der Befragten lebt in kleinen Dörfern und nur wenige wohnen in Städten mit mehr als 100.000 Einwohnern (Graphik 27).
- Das Opferrisiko in Warschau (Polen) entspricht ungefähr demjenigen in Westeuropäischen Grosstädten, aber Taschendiebstähle werden häufiger berichtet. In Surabaja (Indonesien) liegt es besonders bei Autodiebstählen und Angriffen relativ tief (Tabelle 1).
- Die Kriminalitätsbelastung ist in den amerikanischen Städten (mit über 100.000 Inwohnern) im allgemeinen höher als in Städten derselben Grösse in anderen Ländern, wobei es bei einzelnen Delikten Ausnahmen gibt. In europäischen und kanadischen Städten ist die Kriminalitätbelastung ähnlich. Die Belastung der australischen Städte variiert nach Deliktart, liegt aber im allgemeinen tiefer als in kanadischen und amerikanischen Städten.

126

Vergleich zwischen Umfragedaten und der Polizeistatistik

- Bei einem Vergleich der Raten an berichteten Straftaten in den einzelnen Ländern gemäß der vorliegenden Untersuchung und den entsprechenden Raten gemäß der internationalen Kriminalstatistik der INTERPOL zeigten sich eher mässige Rang-Korrelationen. Die beste Uebereinstimmung zeigte sich bei Autodiebstahl, einem besonderes häufig angezeigten Delikt. Bei Raub, tätlichen und sexuellen Angriffen zeigt sich ebenfalls eine grössere übereinstimmung, wenn allein die jenigen Taten berücksichtigt werden, die die Opfer angeblich der Polizei gemeldet haben.
- Da die Daten der vorliegenden Untersuchung nicht von der Anzeigeneigung und der polizeilichen Registrierungspraxis beeinflußt werden, vermitteln sie wahrscheinlich ein zuverlässigeres Bild von der internationalen Kriminalitätsverteilung als die Polizeistatistiken.

Straftaten und ihre Opfer

Soziale Verteilung des Opferrisikos

- Bei den meisten Arten von Straftaten tragen Männer ein höheres Opferrisiko als Frauen, und jüngere Personen ein höheres als Rentner. Ebenso werden die Bewohner größerer Städte überdurchschnittlich häufiger Opfer der hier berüchsichtigten Straftaten. Es scheint, daß das häufige nächtliche Ausgehen junger Männer und Frauen in den Städten das Opferrisiko dieser Bevölkerungsgruppe erhöht (Tabellen 4 und 5).
- In Ländern mit vielen berufstätigen Frauen ist das Verbrechensrisiko für beide Geschlechter relativ ausgeglichen, während in Ländern mit tiefer weiblicher Beschäftigungsquote (Niederlande, Nordirland, Schweiz), das Risiko für Frauen deutlich tiefer liegt als für Männer.

Anzeigeverhalten

- Insgesamt wurden von den berichteten Straftaten in 1988 50% bei der Polizei angezeigt. Dabei zeigten sich allerdings große Unterschiede zwischen den einzelnen Straftaten, wobei vor allem Eigentumsdelikte häufiger angezeigt wurden, so etwa 93% der Autodiebstähle, 77% der Einbrüche, und 60% der Fahrraddiebstähle. Seltener angezeigt wurden Raub (49%), übrige Diebstähle (41%), tätliche Angriffe (31%) und mutwillige Beschädigung von Automobilen (39%). Von den sexuellen Angriffen wurden 10% angezeigt, wobei man im Auge behalten muß, daß die Opfer 69% der berichteten Erlebnisse als nicht unbedingt strafbare "freche Unanständigkeit" einstuften. Gewaltsame sexuelle Angriffe wurden häufiger angezeigt (24%), darunter insbesondere Vergewaltigungen (48%). (Zur Anzeigehäufigkeit nach Delikt und Ländern vgl. die Graphiken 2, 4, 6, 9, 11, 14, 17, 20, 23 und Tabelle E.4).

- Werden alle berichteten Straftaten gesamthaft betrachtet, so zeigten sich verhältnismäßig tiefe Anzeigeraten in Indonesien (18%), Spanien (34%), Polen (41%), Norwegen (43%) und Finnland (45%) (Graphik 33). Personen in der niedrigsten Einkommensklasse haben erlittene Delikte seltener angezeigt als die übrigen Befragten (38% gegenüber 51%).
- Wurden Straftaten nicht angezeigt, so wurde als Begründung hierfür (alle Länder zusammen genommen) am häufigsten erwähnt, daß die Sache "nicht schwerwiegend genug" gewesen sei (40%), daß "die Polizei auch nichts hätte machen können" (19%) oder daß die Polizei "sich nicht darum gekümmert hätte" (10%). Hinsichtlich der Häufigkeit dieser Gründe zeigten sich kaum Unterschiede zwischen den einzelnen Ländern. Es zeigte sich auch ein Zusammenhang zwischen dem Versicherungsschutz gegen Einbrüche (bzw. dessen Verbreitung in den einzelhen Ländern) und dem Auzeigverhalten. Befragte mit Versicherungsschutz zeigen häufiger an (87% gegenüber 65%).
- Die meisten Opfer, die Anzeige erstattet hatten, zeigten sich von der Art ihrer Behandlung durch die Polizei befriedigt (66%). Eher selten befriedigt äußerten sich die Opfer in Polen (20%), Norwegen (33%), Spanien (47%), Frankreich (49%) und Belgien (53%) (Graphik 34). Als Gründe nannten die Unzufriedenen hauptsächlich, daß die Polizei zuwenig unternommen habe (41%) oder "gar nicht interessiert" gewesen sei (41%).

Algemeine Einstellung zur Polizei

- Zwei Drittel der Befragten waren der Ansicht, daß die Polizei ihres Wohnortes "ihre Sache gut mache". Am häufigsten finden dies die Befragten in Kanada (89%), in den Vereinigten Staaten (81%), in Surabaja (76%) und in Australien (73%). Am häufigsten unzufrieden äußerten sich die Befragten in Polen (69%). Ebenfalls eher häufig waren die kritischen Stimmen in Spanien (29%), Deutschland (24%) und Belgien (22%) (Graphik 35).
- Dabei scheint kein Zusammenhang mit dem Ausmaß an Kriminalität in den einzelnen Ländern zu bestehen. Allerdings äußern sich die Opfer von Straftaten (im Jahre 1988) häufiger unzufrieden als die übrigen Befragten (25 gegenüber 16%).

Opferhilfe

- Nur 3.8% der Opfer von Straftaten, die bei der Polizei angezeigt haben erhielten (im Durchschnitt aller Länder) Hilfe von einer Opferberatungsstelle oder einer ähnlichen Einrichtung, die auf praktische und psychologische Hilfe an Opfer von Straftaten spezialisiert ist. Dieser Anteil war in den Vereinigten Staaten (10.0%), in Kanada (5.5%), Belgien (6.4%), Finnland (4.4%) und England und Wales (4.0%) geringfügig höher (Graphik 36).

128

- Dieser Anteil war auch höher bei den Opfern von sexuellen Angriffen (15.1%), Raub (8.6%), Einbruch (7.7%) und Angriffen (7.3%), bei weiblichen Opfer (4.1%) und Personen mit beschiedenem Einkommen (5.8%).
- Wesentlich höher war demgegenüber der Anteil der Opfer, die ihren Angaben zufolge eine solche Hilfe begrüßt hätten (35%); besonders hoch war dieser Anteil in Polen und Indonesien (Graphik 37).
- Am stärksten war der Wunsch nach einer solchen Hilfe bei den Opfern von sexuellen Angriffen, während sich kaum Einflüsse von Geschlecht und Alter zeigten.
- In allen Ländern ist der Anteil derer, die gerne eine solche Hilfe erhalten hätten, weitaus höher als die Zahl der Empfänger entsprechender Hilfeleistungen.

Reaktionen auf Kriminalität

Angst vor Kriminalität

- Gefragt wurde im Rahmen der vorliegenden Untersuchung nach Vorbeugungs- und Vermeidungsstrategien bei abendlichen Ausgängen (Ausgehen nur in Begleitung/Vermeiden gewisser Straßenzüge, um einem Verbrechen vorzubeugen) sowie nach der vermuteten Wahrscheinlichkeit, im Verlaufe der nächsten 12 Monate Opfer eines Wohnungseinbruchs zu werden.
- Dabei zeigte sich, daß die subjektive Einschätzung des Einbruchrisikos eng mit der objektiven Häufigkeit von Einbrüchen im betreffenden Land (Graphik 40) sowie entsprechenden Opfererfahrungen einhergeht.
- Demgegenüber steht die Häufigkeit von Vorbeugungs- und Vermeidungsstrategien mit dem Risiko eines Gewaltdelikts im betreffenden Land in keinem Zusammenhang, obwohl sich international durchaus Unterschiede zeigen (Graphik 38). Besonders verbreitet sind sie in Deutschland, England und Wales, in den USA, sowie in Warschau und Surabaja.
- Allgemein gilt, daß Frauen viel häufiger als Männer solche Vorsichtmaßnahmen ergreifen. Dasselbe gilt für Opfer von Gewaltdelikten (besonders Frauen) im Vergleich zu Nicht-Opfern.

Einstellungen zu Strafen

- Gefragt wurde im Rahmen der vorliegenden Untersuchung nach der angemessenen Strafe für einen 21-jährigen rückfälligen Einbrecher, der einen Farbfernseher gestohlen hat. Im Durchschnitt aller Länder wurde "Verpflichtung zu einer Arbeitsleistung" mit 41 % am häufigsten genannt, vor Gefängnis (28%) und Geldstrafe (13%). Ueberdurchschnittlich häufig sprachen sich die Befragten in Indonesien, in den Vereinigten Staaten, in Polen, Nordirland, Schottland, England und Wales, Australien und Kanada für eine (unbedingte) Freiheitsstrafe aus, wogegen die Verpflichtung zu einer Arbeitsleistung (Community Service Order) in der Bundesrepublik Deutschland (60%), der Schweiz (57%) und in Frankreich (53%) am populärsten zu sein scheint (Tabelle 9).

- Vergleicht man den Anteil der Befragten, die eine unbedingte Freiheitsstrafe für angemessen halten, für jedes Land mit dessen Gefangenenrate (Anzahl Insassen auf 100.000 Einwohner), so zeigt sich eine weitgehende Uebereinstimmung in dem Sinne, daß Länder, wo viele Befragte eine Gefängnisstrafe empfehlen, im allgemeinen auch hohe Gefangenenraten aufweisen (Graphik 41). Höher liegt der Anteil der Befürworter von Freiheitsstrafe für Einbrecher zudem unter den Opfer von Einbrüchen sowie in Ländern mit hoher Einbruchrate.

Präventive Maßnahmen

- Gefragt wurde nach Maßnahmen, die möglicherweise geeignet sind, das Risiko eines Wohnungseinbruchs zu verringern, wie etwa die Anschaffung einer Alarmanlage, die Anstellung eines Hausmeisters (in Wohnblocks) und die Gewohnheit, bei Abwesenheit das Licht brennen zu lassen oder Nachbarn zu verständigen.
- Hinsichtlich der Alarmanlagen zeigte sich ein schwacher Zusammenhang mit dem Risiko eines Einbruchs im betreffenden Land (Graphik 44) in dem Sinne, dass solche Anlagen in Ländern mit hohem Einbruchsrisiko stärker verbreitet sind. Möglicherweise werden derartige Anlagen angeschafft, wenn das Risiko eines Einbruchs - beispielsweise als Folge entsprechender Erfahrungen - als hoch eingeschätzt wird. Sie scheinen im übrigen die Gefahr eines (vollendeten) Einbruchs tatsächlicher etwas zu verringern. Die Verbreitung derartiger Anlagen ist in den einzelnen Ländern sehr unterschiedlich. Ueberdurchschnittlich verbreitet sind sie in England und Wales, Schottland, Belgien, Deutschland, in den Vereinigten Staaten, in Kanada und Australien (Graphik 43).
- Die Verbreitung von Hausmeistern in Mehrfamilienhäusern variiert ebenfalls sehr stark von Land zu Land (Graphik 42), doch wird diese wohl eher von anderen Gesichtspunkten (einschließlich der Tradition) als vom Einbruchsrisiko bestimmt, obwohl Hausmeister neuerdings auch aus solchen Gründen empfohlen werden. Besonders häufig sind sie in den Wohnblocks in den Vereinigten Staaten (57% der befragten Bewohner solcher Häuser), in Kanada (47%) und Australien (32%), aber auch in Frankreich, Finnland, Norwegen und Belgien. Eher selten sind sie in den Niederlanden (12%), Schottland (12%) und in der Schweiz (3%) anzutreffen. In Ländern, wo Hausmeister häufig sind, wie z.B. in Frankreich, zeigen Wohnblocks, die von Hausmeistern überwacht werden, niedrigere Einbruchsraten.
- In verschiedenen Ländern (beispielsweise in den Vereinigten Staaten, England und Wales und Norwegen) ist es üblich, bei Abwesenheit abends in der leeren Wohnung die Lichter brennen zu lassen, wogegen dies anderswo seltener gemacht wird (so etwa in Frankreich, Spanien, Finnland

und in der Schweiz). Möglicherweise hängen diese Unterschiede mit dem in den einzelnen Ländern vorherrschenden Haus- bzw. Wohnungstyp zusammen (Graphik 45).

- Etwas mehr Befragten im Vereinigten Königreich und in den drei aussereuropäischen Ländern pflegen bei längerer Abwesenheit die Nachbarn zu verständigen (Graphik 46). Eine grosse Minderheit - 20% in der Bundesrepublik Deutschland - verzichtet angeblich darauf, weil die Nachbarn ihre Wohnung bei Abwesenheit sowieso überwachen. In den meisten Ländern hatte diese Gruppe das geringste Einbruchrisiko, was die Bedeutung informeller Ueberwachung für die Verbrechensverhütung unterstreicht.

Schlußbemerkungen

Wiewohl die hier zusammengefaßten Ergebnisse der vorliegenden Untersuchung vorderhand einzigartig dastehen und zu verschiedenen Ueberlegungen einladen mögen, ist hier nochmals auf einige ihrer Grenzen hinzuweisen. Wie im Kapitel 1 erläutert, leidet diese Untersuchung an denselben Schwächen, die alle Opferbefragungen auszeichnen, so etwa hinsichtlich der Stichprobenfehler und der Auswahl der berücksichtigten Straftaten, die sich weitgehend auf gewöhnliche und im allgemeinen nicht sehr schwerwiegende Delikte beschränkt.

Um die Teilnahme möglichst vieler Länder zu ermöglichen, wurde zudem Wert auf verhältnismäßig bescheidene Stichproben (und damit geringe Kosten) gelegt, was jedoch zwangsläufig die Stichprobenfehler vergrößert und die Möglichkeit vertiefter Zusatzauswertungen zu Einzelfragen einschränkt. Weitere Unsicherheiten ergeben sich aus der Wahl der telefonischen Befragung, da die Telefondichte nicht in allen Ländern gleich hoch ist. Es ist nicht auszuschließen, daß Personen ohne Telefonanschluß andere Erfahrungen mit und Einstellungen zu Kriminalität haben als die vorliegende Befragten. Ungewiß ist ferner, ob die Bereitschaft, in einer Befragungssituation über Opfererfahrungen zu berichten, in den einzelnen Ländern in unterschiedlichem Maße von kulturellen Vorstellungen (etwa über den Begriff gewisser Straftaten) oder Empfindlichkeiten bei der Kommunikation über heikle Themen dieser Art beeinflußt wird. Letztlich mißt eine Opferbefragung stets mehr die subjektiv wahrgenommene als die tatsächliche Erfahrung mit Kriminalität. Schließlich sei noch darauf hingewiesen, daß die Ergebnisse hier stets auf Landesebene dargestellt werden; es mag sehr wohl sein, daß innerhalb eines Landes ebenso große Unterschiede wie im internationalen Vergleich hinsichtlich des Kriminalitätsrisikos und der Einstellungen bestehen.

Es läßt sich nur schwer beurteilen, inwieweit methodische Probleme dieser Art die dargestellten Ergebnisse beeinflußt haben könnten. Die Mitglieder der Arbeitsgruppe, die das Forschungsvorhaben initiiert hat, neigen zur Ansicht, daß die Verzerrungen nicht allzu schwer ausgefallen sein dürften. Immerhin stimmen viele der mitgeteilten Ergebnisse mit gesicherten kriminologischen Erkenntnissen überein, so etwa die berichteten Zusammenhänge zwischen dem Risiko, Opfer einer Straftat zu werden, und verschiedenen unabhängigen Variablen; sehr weitgehend ist auch die Uebereinstimmung mit herkömmlichen Vorstellungen und kriminologischen Forschungsergebnissen bezüglich des Ausmaßes an Kriminalität in verschiedenen Ländern.

Ein eingehender Forschungsbericht mit verschiedenen vertieften Auswertungen soll in absehbarer Zeit veröffentlicht werden. Die Mitglieder der Arbeitsgruppe würden es auch begrüßen, wenn eine internationale Untersuchung dieser Art zu einem späteren Zeitpunkt in möglichst vielen Ländern erneut durchgeführt werden könnte. Dabei sollten gewisse geringfügigere Verbesserungen der Methodik - aufgrund der Erfahrungen mit der vorliegenden Untersuchung - erwogen werden, wie etwa eine Erweiterung der Stichproben und der Versand einer schriftlichen Ankündigung der (telefonischen) Befragung an die ausgewählten Haushaltungen.

Bis dahin steht der Fragebogen Interessenten in Ländern zur Verfügung die selber eine Opferbefragung planen und die Ergebnisse der vorliegenden Untersuchung gerne zu Vergleichszwecken heranziehen möchten.[2]

---

2. Jaap de Waard, Directie Criminaliteitspreventie, Ministerie van Justitie, 2500 EH Den Haag, Holland.

Annex A Survey methods

Fieldwork execution

Questionnaire and piloting

The questionnaire for the survey was prepared by the Working Group. Comments were received from several academics. The questionnaire was piloted, using CATI, first in the Netherlands and England. Other pilot studies were conducted in France, W.Germany and Finland to test the questionnaire in other languages, and the modifications made after the first pilot. In each country, the questionnaire was piloted with at least 30 respondents. Interviews were conducted in the native language, from the central location of Inter/View in the Netherlands. The Finnish study was carried out by the National Research Institute for Legal Policy in Helsinki.

In the pilot in France, the response effect of two different introductions was measured (30 respondents for each variant). In the first introduction, the name of the sponsor commissioning the survey was mentioned; in the second, this name was not mentioned but rather emphasis was put on the purpose of the survey, and the importance of co-operation. The French test did not show that the type of introduction significantly affected response rates. In view of this, it was left to survey co-ordinators to decide on the type of introduction to be made. In all countries, the questionnaire was introduced as being supported by the sponsor who had commissioned the survey.

The final questionnaire used was an adaptation of the second pilot questionnaire, with some reductions made to its length (to keep it within cost boundaries). The English version was the basis for all translations into other languages. The questionnaire was translated into French, German and Dutch by the Working Group, and these versions were authorised by the national sponsor before fieldwork began. A variety of other arrangements were made for translation into other languages, but in all cases the final version of the questionnaire was agreed with the survey co-ordinator.

Interview briefing and fieldwork attendance

All interviewers were personally briefed by survey personnel. The briefings were done on the basis of a standard list of points to be covered, prepared

133

by the Working Group. In the briefings, the purpose of the survey was explained, as was the structure of the questionnaire. In addition, every effort was made to train interviewers in motivating respondents who initially appeared unwilling to co-operate.

The survey co-ordinators for client countries had the opportunity of attending the interviewer briefings. During the CATI fieldwork, the co-ordinators were able to attend fieldwork once more on appointment. The co-ordinators were requested to provide the name and address of a contact-person who during the fieldwork period could answer respondents' questions about the authenticity of the survey. In several countries this resulted in a substantial number of calls for information from respondents (eg, Canada, England & Wales, Scotland, and Belgium); in most countries, respondents made only incidental use of this telephone number.

Timing of fieldwork

Table A.1 shows the dates of fieldwork in the fourteen main participating countries. In Warsaw (Poland) interviewing took place in February/March 1989. In Surabaja (Indonesia) it took place in the second half of March.

Table A.1: Timing of fieldwork, 1989

England & Wales	16 January	- 25 February
Scotland	18 January	- 25 February
N.Ireland	27 February	- 23 March
Netherlands	11 January	- 31 January
W.Germany	17 January	- 23 February
Switzerland	2 February	- 17 March
Belgium	27 January	- 20 February
France	23 January	- 6 February
Spain	22 February	- 7 April
Norway	31 January	- 26 February
Finland	23 January	- 12 February
USA	14 March	- 18 April
Canada	27 January	- 16 February
Australia	20 January	- 30 January

Telephone penetration

Table A.2 shows levels of telephone penetration in the 14 main participating countries. Up-to-date figures are difficult to obtain. Those in Table A.2 were mainly supplied by companies commissioned to work on the survey by Inter/View. Figures with asterisks derive from a survey of 22 countries carried out by Trewin and Lee (1988), whose estimates seem more in accord with other information collected from country co-ordinators.

134

Table A.2: Telephone penetration: % of households with a telephone

England & Wales[1]	82 - 85
Scotland	82 - 85
N.Ireland	<70
Netherlands	95
W.Germany[3]	>94
Switzerland	97 - 98
Belgium	72 - 75
France	93 - 95
Spain[2]	70 - 73
Norway	92 - 94
Finland[3]	>94
USA	94+
Canada	97
Australia	93

Notes:
1. Where ranges are shown, these are for rural and urban areas respectively.
2. Urban areas only.
3. The Trewin and Lee (1988) figure for W.Germany was 94% in 1985, and for Finland 94% in 1986. Their figure for Canada was 97% in 1986.

Telephone sampling methods

Methods of sampling telephone numbers differed slightly across country according to local arrangements. Table A.3 summarizes the main features.

Table A.3: Telephone survey methods, by country

	United Kingdom[1]	Nether-lands	W.Ger-many	Switzer-land	Belgium	France	Spain	Norway	Finland	USA	Canada	Aus-tralia
Random digit dialling:												
- yes	X[2]	X			X	X	X	X		X	X	
- no			X	X					X			X
Random number generation based on:			n/a	n/a					n/a			n/a
- existing number series	X		X				X		X			
- modified existing number series						X	X			X[3]	X	
Original sample source:												
- most recent telephone directories		X	X	X	X		X	X	X	X[4]	X	X
- sample on tape from tel. companies										X		
- other	X[5]					X						
Resulting sample:												
- fully random representative	X	X	X		X	X	X	X	X	X	X	
- stepwise clustered by areacodes												
- otherwise clustered				X[6]								X
Percentage of unlisted numbers[7]	7	13	1	3[8]	6-7	4	10	1[9]	15[10]	30	15	5

1. Procedures for England & Wales and Scotland were the same.
2. UK: Known numbers were used with the last digit omitted. The last digit was randomly generated, giving in effect a random number, which will cover unlisted numbers. RDD selects randomly from numbers in a known series.
3. USA: Known existing (506) prefixes and (24) banks were pooled and last 2 digits of number were generated.
4. USA: Source for bank generation. Both telephone directories and tape samples were used in the USA.
5. UK: Targeting Database Company provided telephone numbers according to specific (eg, regional) proportions. The database uses up-to-date telephone numbers.
6. Switzerland: Random selection of communities (step 1), random selection of telephone numbers within selected communities (step 2).
7. In countries with random digit dialling, unlisted numbers will have been sampled. All percentages of unlisted numbers are estimates, except for W.Germany. The estimates relate to either 1988 or 1989.
8. Switzerland: A household is not allowed to have an unlisted number unless it possesses several telephones.
9. Norway: Unlisted telephones, less than 1%. Company phones can have a number of lines which are clustered and only one number listed.
10. Finland: 20% in Helsinki area.

136

Response information

CATI response

In general with CATI surveys, there are many sources of non-response. The first category of non-response is *non-relevant contacts* - ie, telephone calls not answered at all, out of the gross sample. The *gross sample* is all telephone numbers which were used at least once. For the purpose of calculating response rates, these non-relevant contacts are disregarded. Instead, the response rate is calculated on the basis of:

$$\frac{\text{completed interviews}}{\text{completed interviews + relevant contacts}}$$

Thereafter, there are various types of non-response, one of which is refusal to be interviewed. The categories of non-response are explained in more detail below.

1. GROSS SAMPLE
   All telephone numbers which were used at least once.

2. NON-RELEVANT CONTACTS
   - repeatedly busy (includes an unknown number of faxes, answering devices)
   - No answer after repeated attempts (includes an unknown number of non-existing telephone numbers)
   - Disconnected (non-existing numbers)
   - Business numbers (non-households)

3. RELEVANT CONTACTS
   3.1 Refusal/terminated interview
   3.2 Other non-contacts
      a. General problem
         - Hearing problem (no interview possible)
         - Language problem (no qualifying household)
      b. Target realized, but no interview
         - Appointment after close of fieldwork
         - Qualified respondent not available during fieldwork
      c. Other reasons
         - Other reasons no interview possible (illness)
         - Interview not valid

4. COMPLETED INTERVIEW
   The average results for the 13 CATI countries are listed below. Table A.4 shows these response figures for the 13 CATI countries separately.

Table A.4: Response information, by country

	final valid sample[1]	gross sample	non-relevant contacts[2]	relevant contacts	not interviewed refusals/ terminated	not interviewed other[3]	completed interviews[1]	non-relevant contacts	relevant contacts refusal terminated	relevant contacts other	response rate valid sample rel. contact
	A	B	C	D	E	F	G	A/B	E/D	F/D	A/D
England & Wales	2006	9802	5085	4717	2290	420	2007	51.9%	48.5%	8.9%	42.5%
Scotland	2007	8836	3980	4856	2350	499	2007	45.0%	48.4%	10.3%	41.3%
Netherlands	2000	6118	3051	3067	744	323	2000	49.9%	24.3%	10.5%	65.2%
W.Germany	5274	20469	2990	17479	10376	1829	5274	14.6%	59.4%	10.5%	30.2%
Switzerland	1000	2050	586	1464	379	84	1001	28.6%	25.9%	5.7%	68.3%
Belgium	2060	9407	3872	5535	2802	665	2068	41.2%	50.6%	12.0%	37.2%
France	1502	7881	4963	2918	844	573	1502	63.0%	28.9%	19.6%	51.5%
Spain[4]	862	5622	3006	2616	1160	594	862	53.5%	44.3%	22.7%	33.0%
Norway	1009	2230	806	1424	255	160	1009	36.1%	17.9%	11.2%	70.9%
Finland	1025	2306	832	1474	378	71	1025	36.1%	25.6%	4.8%	69.5%
USA	1996	10663	5234	5429	2745	688	1996	49.1%	50.6%	12.7%	36.8%
Canada	2074	7225	2432	4793	1916	791	2086	33.7%	40.0%	16.5%	43.3%
Australia	2012	6312	1887	4425	2227	185	2013	29.9%	50.3%	4.2%	45.5%
Average[5]	2000	7609	2979	4631	2190	530	1911	39.1%	47.3%	11.4%	41.3%

1) Data for a small number of interviews was not useable.
2) ie, busy, no answer, disconnected, business numbers.
3) Include (i) language, hearing difficulties; (ii) target realized but respondent not available during fieldwork; (iii) no eligible respondent or invalid interview. For all countries, these problems accounted for 2.1%, 6.0% and 3.4% or non-response respectively.
4) Contact figures based on 862 CATI interviews only. The valid interviews of 2041 in Spain include 1179 face-to-face interviews.
5) Based on weighted data.

1. Gross sample	100.0%
2. Non-relevant contacts	39.1%
3. Relevant contacts	61.9%
3.1 Refusal/terminated	47.3%
3.2 Other non-response	
a. General problem	2.1%
b. Target realised, no interview	6.0%
c. Other reasons	3.4%
4. Completed interviews	41.3%

Refusal rates

Probably the most important type of non-response is where the contacted respondent refuses to be interviewed, or terminates the interview before it is completed. Before the start of fieldwork, the local survey agencies were asked to provide a rough estimate of the refusal rate they expected on the current survey in relation to the refusal rate common in marketing research in their country. Although estimates varied widely, a refusal rate of 20-30% was generally expected. Most agencies expected a refusal rate of the same order as is common in marketing research, or slightly lower. Two (in part counter-balancing) effects were expected. First, it was felt that there might be a negative effect on response due to the sensitivity of the subject matter. Second, it was thought that there might be a positive effect due to the emphasis on the social importance of the survey topic, and the possibility of respondents being able to verify the authenticity of the survey.

In the event, the refusal rate varied widely, from 18% to 59%. Across the board the refusal rate was higher than anticipated. Several reasons for this were mentioned by local fieldwork companies, in particular:
a. In some countries, there is a quickly deteriorating response to telephone research due to an explosive growth in telephone marketing activities. The crime survey could have suffered from this. W.Germany and the USA are especially worth mentioning in this connection.
b. The sensitivity of the research topic in some countries.
c. The data-protection laws and the reaction of the public to these causes problems for all market research in W.Germany

To try and assess the possible bias in results due to refusals, a brief question about victimization experience was inserted early in the questionnaire to be put to people who seemed obviously reluctant to proceed with a full interview. The aim was to see whether, on the basis this early question, refusers tended to admit that they had experienced crime recently or not. In the event, analysis of replies to this question was not helpful. Most refusers terminated the interview before the 'test' victimization question was reached. Most of those who did answer it, said they had not been victims. However, numbers are small and it may well be that these people said they had no experience of crime *in order to* justify why they did not want to continue.

The extent of bias in the results from variable rates of non-response is discussed at the end of this Annex.

Effect of a introductory letter sent to respondents in W.Germany

As an experiment to test the effect on response, an introductory letter was sent to a fresh sample of 500 before they were telephoned. Because fieldwork was nearing the end, the level of non-contacts was higher among those written to than among those who were telephoned (ie, interviewers had limited time to contact someone at home). However, taking this into account, the results indicated that response rates among those contacted were rather higher (43%) than among the main sample not sent a letter (28%). Victimization rates for those receiving a letter were very similar indeed to those for others.

Mention is also made later of another experiment in W.Germany regarding response rates.

Face-to-face interviewing in N.Ireland and Spain

N.Ireland

In N.Ireland, all interviews took place face-to-face. Standard national sampling procedures were used in which interviewers were obliged to conduct a number of interviews according to pre-determined fixed quotas. Quota sampling was chosen instead of stratified random sampling on account of the considerable cost savings. Interviews were conducted from 100 sampling points stratified on the basis of regional data from the Electoral Register. In addition, quotas were set on the basis of age, social class and gender (men, housewives, other women).

Spain

In Spain 1179 interviews were face-to-face, and a further 862 were done through CATI. The *overall* sample was designed to be proportional to the national population aged 16 and over (official 1986 figures), stratified by 17 Autonomical Regions and Habitats (four levels of place of residence size). After drawing the overall sample, rural municipalities and urban areas with low telephone penetration were chosen for face-to-face interviews using five stratification stages (Autonomical Region, Habitat, Municipality, District, and Census Section). Quotas were based on gender, age (5 groups), and activity (employed/unemployed *versus* student, retired, houseperson).

For CATI interviews, the first three stratification stages were used: Autonomical Region, Habitat, and Municipality. (Telephone directories are not divided into District and Census Section.)

Refusals

For face-to-face interviews in N.Ireland and Spain, as interviewers were not working with a fixed list of addresses, it is not possible to determine a non-response rate either due to ineligible addresses, or refusals. (Refusals rates are difficult to obtain because of respondents can refuse to be interviewed before it is known whether they meet the criteria for selection.) However, in N.Ireland rough notes kept by interviewers indicated that on average there was one refusal for each four successful interviews (ie, a refusal rate of about 20%). This level of refusal was considered average. In Spain, refusals in face-to-face interviews were considered by the survey agency to be lower than normal in political and opinion research. This was felt to be because of the sensitivity of the public to the issue of crime, and because of the introductory letter which mentioned the Ministry of Justice as sponsor.

Telephone ownership

As might be imagined, the most important difference between owners and non-owners in different countries relates to household income. This itself reflects in the fact that non-owners are more likely to be, eg, non-white, unemployed, living in rural areas, single-person and elderly households, etc (eg, Massey, 1988). The possible bias from differential telephone ownership ('non-coverage bias') will centre, then, largely on the relationship between income and experience of crime. One test of this from the present data is from the survey in N.Ireland in which all respondents were asked whether or not their household had a telephone. There were no statistically significant differences in victimization risks for telephone owners and non-owners except in relation to theft of and from cars; telephone owners in N.Ireland with a telephone had significantly *higher* risks than non-telephone owners.

Though this is a limited test in one country,[1] it suggests that higher income (as evidenced by having a phone) can be related to higher victimization for some offences. Moreover, other results in Chapter 3 also show a consistent

---

1. In contrast, some analysis (by the authors) of data from the 1985 and 1986 General Household Survey conducted in England & Wales showed that risks of burglary (the only offence asked about) were approximately twice as high among non-telephone owners as among owners; 84% of the sample had telephones.

relationship between income and risk: those with above-average incomes (with and without controlling for vehicles ownership) had higher overall victimization risks, though there was some variation at the level of individual offences. This was the case both at the individual country level, and on the basis of analysis in which data from all the 14 main participating countries were combined.

On the face of it, the results suggest that victimization risks may be somewhat *overestimated* relative to other places in countries with lower telephone ownership - ie, where a larger proportion of non-owners have been omitted from the sample. This would apply to Belgium, England & Wales, and Scotland, although overall risks as measured in these countries were already only moderate. The results would also suggest that the survey has not produced lower estimates of crime than would have been the case with fuller representation of the population. The underrepresentation of low income households is in fact more likely to have resulted in an overestimation of risks. It should be said, though, that this is somewhat contrary to what many researchers would believe (notwithstanding the complex research evidence).[2] Also, comparisons with results from independent surveys do not seem to bear this out.

The tentative conclusion drawn by the authors is that non-coverage bias may not be a substantial problem in interpreting relative and absolute risks. Moreover, the point should be restated that countries in the survey had generally high telephone coverage, and that the range of non-coverage was not great. The samples taken, therefore, were fairly representative of national populations, and the results are unlikely to be greatly affected by any differences in risks insofar as these are income-related.

Response rates

The question of whether the variable response rate in different countries affects the amount of victimization measured is again complicated. Refusal to be interviewed is generally held to be the biggest problem as regards bias, though other forms of non-contact (see above) cannot be overlooked as they may indicate difficulty in achieving interviews with particular types of people

---

2. Analysis of data from victim surveys done in other countries shows no simple relationship between victimization risks and affluence: risks vary by income group in different ways for different crimes, and results across surveys do not always closely match (authors' analysis). Often quoted results from the US National Crime Survey show that risks of personal victimization (robbery, assault etc) are higher among low-income groups (US Department of Justice, 1988). Some household crime, particularly burglary, also hits low-income groups more, though with an increase in risks for the highest income level, and a rather different pattern of results for black Americans. For thefts of cars higher income groups are more vulnerable, no doubt reflecting ownership patterns to some extent These pattern are not always supported in other national surveys: in England and Wales, for instance, burglary risks increase with income (Hough, 1984).

- for instance, those who are ill, or frequently away from home (Collins et al., 1988).[3]

Two small tests in W.Germany have something to say first about non-response bias. One was carried out with the aim of obtaining a higher response rate, and testing whether the victimization experience of non-responders differed from those of responders. Contact was made for a second time with 166 out of 969 people (17%) who had initially refused to be interviewed. The total number of victimizations of all types asked about in the survey which were experienced over 5 years among the re-contacts was 119.4 per 100 people; among the main sample, the figure was 125.5. Though only a relatively small proportion of initial refusers were re-contacted, there is no evidence to suggest that initial refusers had significantly higher or lower victimization rates. This argues against non-response bias, though the results have to be regarded tentatively. It should also be noted that the re-contacted group had a higher average age, had left school earlier (reflecting age), and lived more often in urban areas. The higher average age will depress victimization risks, while the fact that they lived more often in urban centres will increase it.

Another test in W.Germany indicated that interviewers themselves varied very greatly in the success they had in achieving interviews with selected respondents. Interviewer performance, then, could be more relevant to response than differences between responders and non-responders, though only full information from all countries would confirm this.

One argument about response bias, in particular refusal bias, is that victims will be over-represented among responders. The topic of the research will be more salient to them, and they will be more willing to be interviewed *because they had been victimized*. This would have the effect of overestimating victimization risks in countries were response was poorer. Some earlier research in the Netherlands (Fiselier, 1978, on the basis of a mail questionnaire) and in Switzerland (Killias, 1989) lends support to this. Both studies showed that victimization rates were slightly higher among respondents than among non-respondents - though the differences were small. A contrary argument is that with low response rates, people are omitted with whom it is harder to achieve an interview: people who may be more liable to victimization because they are residentially more unstable, if

---

3. In this cross-national survey, it may be that the contribution of 'other non-contacts' is more complex as regards response rates. Survey companies would inevitably have followed slightly different practices in different countries, so that non-contact other than through refusal may have been due more to fieldwork, or interviewer factors than to the characteristics of those not contacted. Refusal was the biggest element of non-response in all countries, though its importance varied somewhat. For instance, 92% of non-contacts in Australia were people who refused to be interviewed, whereas at the other end of the scale, only 60% were refusers in France. There was very little relationship between the two forms of non-response (r=.011): countries with high refusals were far from being consistently those who high levels of other non-contact.

not simply away from home more. There is some evidence bearing on this point from non-response studies outside the victimization field, which suggest that non-responders register higher on 'negative' social indicators, such as ill-health (eg, Groves and Lyberg, 1988).

Data from the present survey does not support either position unequivocally. Victimization risks were generally higher in countries with the highest non-response (eg, the USA, Spain, W.Germany). On the face of it, this would appear to support the first argument that victims were over-represented and that risks in low response countries have been correspondingly overstated. However, the relationship was not statistically strong, and intuitively it is not wholly persuasive.[4] Risks in Holland, for instance, have been shown to be very high in the survey, though non-response, and refusal in particular, was comparatively very low; in Belgium, non-response was high but risks low. It would also seem surprising if risks in the US were actually lower than have been indicated, which would be the case according to this position.

However, there is no strong support either for the contrary argument that low response rates indicate an under-representation of victims, and as a corollary of this that high response rates lead to a relative overestimation of risks. Certainly, the survey confirms that those with an active social life are more at risk of some crimes, but being away from home frequently will be only one factor explaining non-contact. And again it offends intuition to think that risks in Norway, Finland and Switzerland are overestimated in the survey relatively speaking - when in fact these countries where characterized by noticeably low risks already.

In brief, then, the authors conclude that there is no clear evidence on the effects of non-response. This suggests it may not be an important factor in biasing the results. It is not ruled out that there could possibly be counterbalancing effects operating, such that the survey picked up a proportion of over-victimized respondents, but lost others for different reasons. Nor can it be ruled out, of course, that the effects of non-response worked differently in different countries. In the US, for instance, there may have been a particular problem in reaching high-risk groups (such as blacks in inner cities), though non-whites in general were not underrepresented in the sample.

---

4. The rank order correlations between non-response rates and overall victimization risks was not statistically significant ($r=.591$; $n=13$). The correlation between refusal rates and victimization was .503. At the level of individual offences, the correlations were weaker. N.Ireland was excluded from analysis because of missing response information. Response information for Spain related only to those interviewed through CATI.

Annex B Weighting procedure

1 Need for weighting results (households versus individuals)

In each randomly selected telephone household only one randomly selected respondent aged 16 or over was interviewed. No substitution of the selected respondent with another member of the household was allowed. This procedure guarantees the high quality of the sample and eliminates the disadvantage of quota sampling - that the most cooperative respondents within a household are interviewed.

People in households of different size have different probabilities of being chosen for interview, and weighting is needed to correct for this in order to generate a representative 'persons' sample. For instance, in a household of one person, this person will always be interviewed, while in a household comprising five persons of 16 years or older, the chance of their being interviewed is only one in five. In the latter household, the selected respondent will represent all five persons and his/her answers need to be treated with a corresponding weight. Otherwise, respondents from small households would be over-represented when respondents are selected from within households, but information is needed at the personal level. Weighting of the results, then, is done to give the number of people in households of different sizes the weight of their proportion in the population.

Apart from household-to-person translation, which is made by weighting, corrections were also made to make the samples as representative as possible in terms of gender, age, and regional distribution.

2 Weighting procedure: methodology

For each country, the most recent statistics about how many of the population were in households of different size were used as a reference. Additional input for the weighting procedure concerned population, gender, age and regional population distribution. (No appropriate international statistics are available on other criteria such as income, urbanization, tenure, etc., to enable them to be used in weighting.) In most countries, appropriate statistics concerning how the population of those *16 years and older* ('adults') was distributed within households of different size was either unavailable, or inadequate. Thus, these statistics were derived from the present survey itself.

How the household weight was computed

First, on the basis of the available statistics on how many of the population were in households of different size, the total sample in each country was weighted according to the ideal *household sample*, correctly distributed according to region and gender. This was done in an iterative weighting procedure in which individual respondent weights were computed to achieve a weighted result with marginal totals on gender and region, corresponding to population distributions (see the calculations in Example 1). Once this was done, additional weighting was done in a similar way to correct for possible distortions in the distribution of the sample according to household size.

In the survey itself, the composition of the households was determined by asking each respondent how many persons the household as a whole consisted of, and also how many of those persons were 16 years or older.

The computation of the distribution of persons 16+ within household size

Using the weighted results on the distribution of adults in households of different size, it was then possible to determine for each country how many adults form part of households of different sizes (see the calculations in Example 2). The number of adults thus calculated was compared to comparable population statistics where these were available, and no significant deviations were found. In view of this, it was decided to follow the same procedure for all the countries, and the survey calculations were used as the weighting criterion for the *person weight*.

Calculation of the person weight

In addition to the procedures outlined above, age also served as input in the final step of the person weight. (This was done at the request of the Working Group to correct for minor differences in the age distribution of the samples - age being an important correlate of victimization risk. Statistics on age the following age-groups were used: 16-34; 35-49; 50-64; 65 and older.) The basis for the person weight, then, were procedures used to calculate the household weight (see Step 1 below). The person weight was computed by the same iterative process as described for the household weight, with marginal totals for gender, region, number of adults per household, and age serving as criteria.

As individual respondents were seen as both representative of a household sample *and* a sample of adults, each data record basically contains two weighting factors, ie, a household weight and a person weight.[1] The weighting procedure can be summarized as follows:

step 1   weighting according to the ideal *household sample* on the basis of available population statistics regarding household size, region and gender

step 2   deriving the population data concerning the distribution of adults according to household size

step 3   weighting according to *persons sample* on the basis of figures derived in Step 2, gender, region and age

The resulting sample is one which can be used to analyse household data (Step 1), and also used as a persons-sample (Step 3). The results in this report have been based on the personal weight.

---

1. To facilitate different kinds of analysis, the data tape contains a household and personal weight for three totals:
   1. the net sample (different from country to country);
   2. the standardized sample size of N=2,000 (for inter-country comparisons); and
   3. the population in thousands (households) and ten-thousands (persons).

Example 1

Example calculation weights international crime survey

Values Sample:	region			Description of cells Sample:	region			Comment
sex	north	south	total	sex	north	south	total	(1)
- male	300	500	800	- male	a	d	g	
- female	400	800	1200	- female	b	e	h	
total	700	1300	2000	total	c	f	i	

Population:	region			Population:	region			
sex	north	south	total	sex	north	south	total	(2)
- male	?	?	6000	- male	A	D	G	
- female	?	?	8000	- female	B	E	H	
total	5000	9000	14000	total	C	F	I	

Weight for sex:		Weight for sex:			
sex		sex		formula	(3)
- male	1.07	- male	J	$J=(G/I)/(g/i)$	
- female	0.95	- female	K	$K=(H/I)/(h/i)$	

Weight for region:	region		Weight for region:	region		
	north	south total		north	south	formula (4)
	1.02	0.99		L	M	$L=(C/I)/(c/i)$
						$M=(f/I)/(f/i)$

Weight per cell:	region		Weight per cell:	region		$N=JxL$ (5)
sex	north	south	sex	north	south	$O=KxL$
- male	1.09	1.06	- male	N	P	$P=JxM$
- female	0.97	0.94	- female	O	Q	$Q=KxM$

Weighted result per cell:	region			Weighted result per cell:	region		
sex	north	south	total	sex	north	south	
- male	328	530	858	- male	Nxa	Pxd	(6)
- female	389	754	1142	- female	Oxb	Qxe	
total	717	1283	2000				(7)

1) This is the distribution of the sample on two variables: sex and region and the combination of these.
2) This is the distribution of the population on the same two variables. Marginals are known, but cell entries are unknown.
3) Calculation of the weighting factor for sex is made.
4) Calculation of the weighting factor for region is made.
5) Calculation of the weighting factor for individual cells: multiplication of the two weighting factors per cell, region and sex.
6) Calculation of the weighted distribution of the sample: cell contents are multiplied with cell weighting factor.
7) For three variables the method is the same, thus multiplication of the weighting factors of each weighting variable.

148

Example 2

Example of calculations of the distribution within householdsize of persons aged 16 years and older.

Sample result:

Cross tabulation weighted for householdsize

number of persons aged 16+ in the household	total	total number of persons in the household			
		1 pers.	2 pers.	3 pers.	4 pers.
1 pers.	800	200	300	200	100
2 pers.	800	400	300	100	
3 pers.	300	200	100		
4 pers.	100		100		
total households	2000	200	700	700	400
Percentage A	100%	10.0%	35.0%	35.0%	20%
Total pers. 16+	3700	200	1100	1400	1000
Percentage B	100.0%	5.4%	29.7%	37.8%	27.0%

Percentage B is calculated by multiplying each frequency in the table by the number of persons in the horizontal row. Figures are then summed per column.
The result is a sample of 2,000 households that represent 3,700 adults, distributed within household size according to percentage B.

Annex C Statistical significance

NOMOGRAM

DEVIATIONS WITHIN A NORMAL DISTRIBUTION WITH A 95% CERTAINTY GIVEN

	P = FOUND PERCENTAGE																	
N— EXTENT OF SAMPLE TAKEN AT RANDOM	0.2 / 99.8	0.5 / 99.5	1 / 99	2 / 98	3 / 97	4 / 96	5 / 95	6 / 94	7-8 / 92-93	9-10 / 90-91	11-12 / 88-89	13-15 / 85-87	16-18 / 82-84	19-22 / 78-81	23-26 / 74-77	27-31 / 69-73	32-40 / 60-68	41-59
22	—	—	—	—	—	13.5	13.9	14.4	15.0	15.7	16.4	17.2	18.0	18.8	19.5	20.2	20.9	21.3
24	—	—	—	—	12.1	12.6	13.1	13.5	14.1	14.9	15.6	16.3	17.1	17.9	18.7	19.3	20.0	20.5
27	—	—	—	—	11.1	11.6	12.0	12.5	13.1	13.8	14.5	15.2	16.0	16.8	17.5	18.2	18.9	19.3
30	—	—	—	—	10.2	10.7	11.2	11.6	12.2	13.0	13.6	14.4	15.1	15.9	16.6	17.2	17.9	18.4
33	—	—	—	—	9.5	10.0	10.5	10.9	11.5	12.2	12.9	13.6	14.3	15.1	15.8	16.4	17.1	17.5
36	—	—	—	8.4	8.9	9.4	9.9	10.3	10.9	11.6	12.2	12.9	13.7	14.4	15.1	15.7	16.4	16.8
40	—	—	—	7.7	8.2	8.7	9.2	9.6	10.2	10.9	11.5	12.2	12.9	13.6	14.3	14.9	15.5	16.0
45	—	—	—	7.0	7.6	8.0	8.5	8.9	9.5	10.1	10.7	11.4	12.1	12.8	13.4	14.0	14.6	15.1
50	—	—	—	6.5	7.0	7.5	7.9	8.3	8.9	9.5	10.1	10.8	11.4	12.1	12.7	13.3	13.9	14.3
55	—	—	—	6.0	6.5	7.0	7.4	7.8	8.4	9.0	9.6	10.2	10.9	11.5	12.1	12.6	13.2	13.6
60	—	—	—	5.6	6.1	6.6	7.0	7.4	7.9	8.6	9.1	9.7	10.4	11.0	11.6	12.1	12.7	13.0
66	—	—	—	5.2	5.7	6.2	6.6	7.0	7.5	8.1	8.6	9.2	9.8	10.4	11.0	11.5	12.1	12.4
73	—	—	4.3	4.9	5.4	5.8	6.2	6.6	7.1	7.6	8.2	8.7	9.3	9.9	10.4	10.9	11.5	11.8
80	—	—	4.0	4.5	5.0	5.5	5.8	6.2	6.7	7.3	7.8	8.3	8.9	9.4	9.9	10.4	10.9	11.3
90	—	—	3.6	4.2	4.6	5.1	5.4	5.8	6.2	6.8	7.3	7.8	8.3	8.9	9.4	9.8	10.3	10.6
100	—	—	3.3	3.9	4.3	4.7	5.1	5.4	5.9	6.4	6.9	7.4	7.9	8.4	8.9	9.3	9.8	10.1
120	—	—	2.9	3.4	3.8	4.2	4.6	4.9	5.3	5.8	6.2	6.7	7.1	7.6	8.1	8.5	8.9	9.2
140	—	—	2.6	3.1	3.5	3.8	4.2	4.5	4.8	5.3	5.7	6.1	6.6	7.0	7.4	7.8	8.2	8.5
170	—	1.9	2.2	2.7	3.1	3.4	3.7	4.0	4.3	4.8	5.1	5.5	5.9	6.3	6.7	7.1	7.4	7.7
200	—	1.7	2.0	2.4	2.8	3.1	3.4	3.6	4.0	4.4	4.7	5.1	5.5	5.8	6.2	6.5	6.8	7.1
250	—	1.4	1.7	2.1	2.4	2.7	3.0	3.2	3.5	3.9	4.2	4.5	4.9	5.2	5.5	5.8	6.1	6.3
300	—	1.2	1.5	1.9	2.2	2.5	2.7	2.9	3.2	3.5	3.8	4.1	4.4	4.7	5.0	5.3	5.6	5.8
350	—	1.1	1.3	1.7	2.0	2.3	2.5	2.7	2.9	3.2	3.5	3.8	4.1	4.4	4.6	4.9	5.1	5.3
400	.8	1.0	1.2	1.6	1.9	2.1	2.3	2.5	2.7	3.0	3.3	3.5	3.8	4.1	4.3	4.6	4.8	5.0
500	.7	.8	1.1	1.4	1.6	1.9	2.0	2.2	2.4	2.7	2.9	3.1	3.4	3.6	3.9	4.1	4.3	4.4
700	.5	.7	.9	1.1	1.4	1.5	1.7	1.8	2.0	2.3	2.4	2.6	2.9	3.1	3.3	3.4	3.6	3.8
1.000	.4	.5	.7	.9	1.1	1.3	1.4	1.5	1.7	1.9	2.0	2.2	2.4	2.6	2.7	2.9	3.0	3.1
1.500	.3	.4	.6	.8	.9	1.0	1.1	1.2	1.4	1.5	1.6	1.8	1.9	2.1	2.2	2.3	2.4	2.6
2.000	.2	.4	.5	.6	.8	.9	1.0	1.1	1.2	1.3	1.4	1.5	1.7	1.8	1.9	2.0	2.1	2.2
3.000	.2	.3	.4	.5	.6	.7	.8	.9	1.0	1.1	1.2	1.3	1.4	1.5	1.6	1.6	1.7	1.8
5.000	.1	.2	.3	.4	.5	.6	.6	.7	.7	.8	.9	1.0	1.1	1.1	1.2	1.3	1.3	1.4
10.000	.1	.1	.2	.3	.3	.4	.4	.5	.5	.6	.6	.7	.7	.8	.8	.9	.9	1.0

Annex D   The International Victimization Survey Questionnaire

Preliminary interview with person who answers the phone after random dialling

Note down sex of interviewer   O   male   O   female

I am an interviewer of the survey company   . We are holding a survey at the
request of   about the views of the public about crime and crime control.

This survey is part of an international project which is being done in all major European
countries, and the USA, Canada and Australia. May I ask you a few general questions? This
interview won't take much of your time. Your answers will, of course, be treated confidentially
and anonymously.

If respondent is suspicious or doubtful. If you want to check whether this survey is done for the
                    or if you would like more information, I can give you the phone-number of someone
at

If respondent asks for that number. His/her telephone number is   . May I call you
back in 30 minutes? *(Supervisor will give number of contactperson at Ministry if necessary).*

If non-response: have you yourself or your household, ever been the victim of crime?

In order to determine which person in your household I must interview, I would like to know
how many persons there are in your household.
(Interviewer: must include respondent and any children).
0   1 person
0   2 persons
0   3 persons
0   4 persons
0   5 persons
0   6 persons
0   7 persons
0   8 persons
0   9 persons
0   10 persons or more

And how many of these are aged 16 or over?
0   1 person
0   2 persons
0   3 persons
0   4 persons
0   5 persons
0   6 persons
0   7 persons
0   8 persons
0   9 persons
0   10 persons or more
0   none

153

How many persons aged under 16 does your household have?

0 1 child
0 2 children
0 3 children
0 4 children
0 5 children
0 6 children
0 7 children
0 8 children
0 9 children
0 10 children or more
0 none

Can you tell me which of the following peope aged 16 or over are in your household?
(Interviewer: read out there will be ... people altoghether).
0 head of family (male)
0 head of family (female)
0 one daughter of 16 years or more
0 several daughters of 16 years or more
0 one son of 16 years or more
0 several sons of 16 years or mor
0 another man living in the house
0 another woman living in the house

Interviewer: note down sex of selected respondent.
(Selection of respondent done randomly by computer programme.)
0 male
0 female

According to my instructions I have to interview the   in your household.
Can you please ask her/him whether he/she is willing to come to the phone?
If not available. Can you tell me at what time I have the best chance of getting him/her on the phone?

Questions to member of household selected by computer.
If other than first contact:

I am an interviewer of the survey company   . We are holding a survey at the request of   about the views of the public about crime and crime control. This survey is part of an international project which is being done in all major European countries, the USA, Canada and Australia. May I please ask you some questions about this? This interview won't take much of your time. Your answers will, of course, be treated confidentially and anonymously.
If respondent is suspicious or doubtful.: If you want to check whether this survey is done for the   , I can give you the phone number of someone at
who can give you more information.
If respondent insists to know: Our contact at   is   . His/her phone number is   . May I call you back in 30 minutes?

1. Has anyone in your household had for private use any of the following types of vehicles over the last year?
   Interviewer: count total number of vehicles at the same time.
   a. **a car, van or truck**
      If yes: **how many most of the time**   Y/N
         Coding: (1, 2, 3, 4, 5 and more)
   b. **a moped, scooter, motorcycle (or mofa)***   Y/N
      (*) only if relevant in country
         If yes: **how many most of the time**
         Coding: (1, 2, 3, 4, 5 and more)

154

c. **a bicycle** *(Interviewer: include children's bicycles)*   Y/N
    If yes: **how many most of the time**
    Coding: (1, 2, 3, 4, 5 and more)

If no car/van, continue with question 5
If no car/moped etc., continue with question 6
If no car/moped or bicycle, continue with question 7

I now want to ask you about crimes you or your household may have experienced during the past five years. It is sometimes difficult to remember such incidents so I will read there questions slowly and I would like you to think carefully about them.

2. *If cars/vans/trucks (yes at question 1a),* **in the past five years have you or other members of your household had any of their cars/vans/trucks stolen? Please take your time to think about this.**
  O yes
  O no
  O don't know

(to car/van/truck owners only)
3. **Apart from this, over the past five years have you or have members of your household been the victim of a theft of a car radio, or something else which was left in your car, or theft of a part of the car, such as a car mirror or wheel?**
(Interviewer: vandalism must not be reported here, but under next question; if the car itself was stolen as well, other thefts must not be reported here).
  O yes
  O no
  O don't know

4. *If cars/vans/trucks,* **apart from thefts, have parts of any of the cars/vans/trucks belonging to your household been deliberately damaged (vandalized) over the past five years?**
(Interviewer: if person thinks it is deliberate, it will count. Traffic accidents should not be reported).
  O yes
  O no
  O don't know

If no moped etc., continue with question 6.
5. **Over the past five years have you or other members of your household had any of their mopeds/scooters/motorcycles/(mofa's)* stolen?**
(*) If relevant in country.
  O yes
  O no
  O don't know

6. **Over the past five years have you or other members of your household had any of their bicycles stolen?**
(Interviewer: include children's bicycles)
  O yes
  O no
  O don't know

7. **Disregarding thefts from garages, sheds or lock-ups, over the past five years, did anyone actually get into your house or flat without permission, and steal or try to steal something?**
(Interviewer: do not count burglaries in second houses).
  O yes
  O no
  O don't know

8. Apart from this, over the past five years, do you have any evidence that someone tried to get into your house or flat unsuccessfully. For example, damage to locks, doors or windows or scratches around the lock?
   O yes
   O no
   O don't know

Next I want to ask you some questions about what may have happened to you personally. Things that you have mentioned already or which happened to other members of your household must not be mentioned now.

9. Over the past five years, has anyone taken something from you by using force or threatening you or did anyone try to do so?
   (Interviewer: pickpocketing must be reported under 10)
   O yes
   O no
   O don't know

(interviewer: read slowly)
10. Besides robberies there are many other types of theft of personal property, such as pickpocketing or the theft of a purse, wallet, clothing, jewellery, sports equipment at one's work, at school or pub or in the street. Over the past five years, have you personally been the victim of any of these thefts?
   O yes
   O no
   O don't know

11. I would now like to ask you some questions about crimes of violence of which you personally may have been the victim.
   (Women only)
   Firstly, a rather personal question. People sometimes grab or touch others for sexual reasons in a really offensive way. This can happen either inside one's house or elsewhere, for instance in a pub, the street, at school or at one's workplace. Over the past five years has anyone done this to you? Please take your time to think about it.
   O yes
   O no
   O don't know

12. Apart from the incidents just covered, have you over the past five years been personally attacked or threatened by someone in a way that really frightened you, either at home or elsewhere, such as in a pub, in the street, at school or at your workplace?
   (Interviewer: include here sexual violence against men, if mentioned by respondent).
   O yes
   O no
   O don't know

Could I now go back to ask you about the crimes you said that happened to you.

13a. First of all, you have said you had been the victim of a theft of a car *(yes at question 2)*. When did this happen? Was it last year, that is in 1988?
   If no, was it before 1988 or was it in 1989?
   (Interviewer: if respondent has been a victim more than once, ask if this happened at least one time in 1988).
   O yes, in 1988 (at least one time)
   O no, only before 1988
   O no, only in 1989
   O don't know

156

13b. *If no,* **how often did it happen in 1988?**
- O once
- O twice
- O three times
- O four times
- O five times or more
- O don't know

(Interviewer: if more times, ask about the last time this ever happened).

13c. **The last time, did this theft happen near your own home, elsewhere in your town or city or local area, elsewhere in the country, or abroad?**
- O near own home
- O elsewhere in the city or local area
- O elsewhere in the country
- O abroad
- O don't know

13d. **The last time, was the car/van ever recovered?**
- O yes
- O no
- O don't know

13e. **The last time, did you or anyone else report the incident to the police?**
- O yes
- O no
- O don't know

13f. *If not,* **why didn't you report it?**
(Interviewer: multiple responses allowed).
If no clear answer: **can you tell me a little more?**
- O not serious enough/no loss/kid's stuff
- O solved it myself/perpetrator known to me
- O inappropriate for police/police not necessary
- O reported to other authorities instead
- O no insurance
- O police could do nothing/lack of proof
- O police won't do anything about it
- O fear/dislike of the police/no involvement wanted with police
- O didn't dare (for fear of reprisal)
- O other reasons
- O don't know

14a. *Victims of theft from car (yes at question 3),* **the theft from your car that you mentioned, when did this happen, was it in 1988?**
If no, **Was it before 1988 or was it in 1989?**
(Interviewer: if respondent has been victim more than once, ask if this happened at least one time in 1988.)
- O yes, in 1988 (at least one time)
- O no, only before 1988
- O no, only in 1989
- O don't know

14b. **How often did it happen in 1988?**
- O once
- O twice
- O three times
- O four times
- O five times or more
- O don't know

157

(Interviewer: if more times, ask about last time this ever happened).

14c. **The last time, did this theft happen near your own home, elsewhere in your town or city or local area, elsewhere in the country or abroad?**
O near own home
O elsewhere in the city or local area
O elsewhere in the country
O abroad
O don't know

14d. **The last time, what was the estimated value of the stolen property, including repair costs?**
(Interviewer: rough estimate)

14e. **The last time, did you or anyone else report that incident to the police?**
O yes
O no
O don't know

14f. *If not,* **why didn't you report it?**
(Interviewer: multiple responses allowed).
If no clear answer: **can you tell me a little more?**
O not serious enough/no loss/kid's stuff
O solved it myself/perpetrator known to me
O inappropriate for police/police not necessary
O reported to other authorities instead
O no insurance
O police could do nothing/lack of proof
O police won't do anything about it
O fear/dislike of the police/no involvement wanted with police
O didn't dare (for fear of reprisal)
O other reasons
O don't know

15a. *Damage to car (yes at question 4),* **the damage you mentioned that was done to your vehicle, when did this happen? Was it in 1988?**
If no, **was it before 1988 or was it in 1989?**
(Interviewer: if respondent has been a victim more than once, ask if this happened at least one time in 1988.
O yes, in 1988 (at least one time)
O no, only before 1988
O no, only in 1989
O don't know

15b. *If 1988,* **how often did it happen in 1988?**
O once
O twice
O three times
O four times
O five times or more
O don't know

(Interviewer: if more times, ask about last time this ever happened).

15c. **The last time, did this theft happen near your own home, elsewhere in your town or city or local area, elsewhere in the country or abroad?**
O near own home
O elsewhere in the city or local area
O elsewhere in the country
O abroad
O don't know

158

15d. **The last time, what was the estimated value of the damage?**
(Interviewer: a rough estimate)

15e. **The last time, did you or someone else report that incident to the police?**
- O yes
- O no
- O don't know

15f. *If not,* **why didn't you report it?**
(Interviewer: multiple responses allowed).
If no clear answer: **can you tell me a little more?**
- O not serious enough/no loss/kid's stuff
- O solved it myself/perpetrator known to me
- O inappropriate for police/police not necessary
- O reported to other authorities instead
- O no insurance
- O police could do nothing/lack of proof
- O police won't do anything about it
- O fear/dislike of the police/no involvement wanted with police
- O didn't dare (for fear of reprisal)
- O other reasons
- O don't know

16a. **You mentioned before the theft of your moped/scooter/motorcycle/mofa. When did this happen, was it in 1988?**
If no, **was it before 1988 or was it in 1989?**
(Interviewer: if respondent has been a victim more than once, ask if this happened at least one time in 1988.
- O yes, in 1988 (at least one time)
- O no, only before 1988
- O no, only in 1989
- O don't know

16b. *If 1988,* **how often did it happen in 1988?**
- O once
- O twice
- O three times
- O four times
- O five times or more
- O don't know

(Interviewer: if more times, ask about last time this ever happened).

16c. **The last time, did this theft happen near your own home, elsewhere in your town or city or local area, elsewhere in the country or abroad?**
- O near own home
- O elsewhere in the city or local area
- O elsewhere in the country
- O abroad
- O don't know

16d. **The last time, was the moped/scooter ever recovered?**
- O yes
- O no
- O don't know

16e. **The last time, did you or anyone else report that incident to the police?**
- O yes
- O no
- O don't know

159

16f. *If not,* **why didn't you report it?**
(Interviewer: multiple responses allowed).
If no clear answer: **can you tell me a little more?**
O not serious enough/no loss/kid's stuff
O solved it myself/perpetrator known to me
O inappropriate for police/police not necessary
O reported to other authorities instead
O no insurance
O police could do nothing/lack of proof
O police won't do anything about it
O fear/dislike of the police/no involvement wanted with police
O didn't dare (for fear of reprisal)
O other reasons
O don't know

17a. **The bicycle theft you mentioned, when did this happen, was it within 1988? ago?**
If no, **was it before 1988 or was it in 1989?**
(Interviewer: if respondent has been a victim more than once, ask if this happened at least one time in 1988.
O yes, in 1988 (at least one time)
O no, only before 1988
O no, only in 1989
O don't know

17b. *If 1988,* **how often did it happen in 1988?**
O once
O twice
O three times
O four times
O five times or more
O don't know

(Interviewer: if more times, ask about last time this ever happened).
17c. **The last time, did this theft happen near your own home, elsewhere in your town or city or local area, elsewhere in the country or abroad?**
O near own home
O elsewhere in the city or local area
O elsewhere in the country
O abroad
O don't know

17d. **The last time, was the bicycle ever recovered?**
O yes
O no
O don't know

17e. **The last time, did you or anyone else report that incident to the police?**
O yes
O no
O don't know

160

17f. *If not,* **why didn't you report it?**
   (Interviewer: multiple responses allowed).
   If no clear answer: **can you tell me a little more?**
   O   not serious enough/no loss/kid's stuff
   O   solved it myself/perpetrator known to me
   O   inappropriate for police/police not necessary
   O   reported to other authorities instead
   O   no insurance
   O   police could do nothing/lack of proof
   O   police won't do anything about it
   O   fear/dislike of the police/no involvement wanted with police
   O   didn't dare (for fear of reprisal)
   O   other reasons
   O   don't know

18a. **The burglary you mentioned, when did this happen, was it within 1988?**
   If no, was it before 1988 or was it in 1989?
   (Interviewer: if respondent has been a victim more than once, ask if this happened at least one time in 1988.
   O   yes, in 1988 (at least one time)
   O   no, only before 1988
   O   no, only in 1989
   O   don't know

18b. *If 1988,* **how often did it happen in 1988?**
   O   once
   O   twice
   O   three times
   O   four times
   O   five times or more
   O   don't know

   (Interviewer: if respondent victim more than once, ask about last incident).
18c. **The last time, was anything actually stolen?**
   If yes, **what do you estimate roughly was the value of the property stolen?**

18d. **The last time, was there any damage?**
   If yes, **what do you estimate roughly was the value of the damage done?**
   (Interviewer: rough estimate).

18e. **Did you or anyone else report the last incident to the police?**
   O   yes
   O   no
   O   don't know

18f. *If not,* **why didn't you report it?**
   (Interviewer: multiple responses allowed).
   If no clear answer: **can you tell me a little more?**
   O   not serious enough/no loss/kid's stuff
   O   solved it myself/perpetrator known to me
   O   inappropriate for police/police not necessary
   O   reported to other authorities instead
   O   no insurance
   O   police could do nothing/lack of proof
   O   police won't do anything about it
   O   fear/dislike of the police/no involvement wanted with police
   O   didn't dare (for fear of reprisal)
   O   other reasons
   O   don't know

161

19a. **The attempted burglary you mentioned, when did this happen, was it in 1988?**
If no, **was it before 1988 or was it in 1989?**
(Interviewer: if respondent has been a victim more than once, ask if this happened at least one time in 1988.
O yes, in 1988 (at least one time)
O no, only before 1988
O no, only in 1989
O don't know

20a. **The theft involving force that you mentioned, when did this happen, was it in 1988?**
If no, **was it before 1988 or was it in 1989?**
(Interviewer: if respondent has been a victim more than once, ask if this happened at least one time in 1988.
O yes, in 1988 (at least one time)
O no, only before 1988
O no, only in 1989
O don't know

20b. *If 1988,* **how often did it happen in 1988?**
O once
O twice
O three times
O four times
O five times or more
O don't know

(Interviewer: if more times, ask about last time this ever happened).

20c. **The last time, did this theft happen near your own home, elsewhere in your town or city or local area, elsewhere in the country or abroad?**
O near own home
O elsewhere in the city or local area
O elsewhere in the country
O abroad
O don't know

20d. **Did the offender have a knife, a gun, another weapon or something the offender used as a weapon?**
If yes, **what was it?**
O knife
O gun
O other weapon/stick
O something used as a weapon
O no weapon
O don't know

20e. **Did the offender actually steal something from you?**
If yes, **what do you estimate roughly the value of the stolen property to be?**
(Interviewer: rough estimate).

20f. **Did you or anyone else report the last incident to the police?**
O yes
O no
O don't know

20g. *If not,* **why didn't you report it?**
    (Interviewer: multiple responses allowed).
    If no clear answer: **can you tell me a little more?**
    O   not serious enough/no loss/kid's stuff
    O   solved it myself/perpetrator known to me
    O   inappropriate for police/police not necessary
    O   reported to other authorities instead
    O   no insurance
    O   police could do nothing/lack of proof
    O   police won't do anything about it
    O   fear/dislike of the police/no involvement wanted with police
    O   didn't dare (for fear of reprisal)
    O   other reasons
    O   don't know

21a. **The theft of personal property that you mentioned, when did this happen, was it in 1988?**
    If no, **was it before 1988 or was it in 1989?**
    (Interviewer: if respondent has been a victim more than once, ask if this happened at least one time in 1988).
    O   yes, in 1988 (at least one time)
    O   no, only before 1988
    O   no, only in 1989
    O   don't know

21b. *If 1988,* **how often did it happen in 1988?**
    O   once
    O   twice
    O   three times
    O   four times
    O   five times or more
    O   don't know

    (Interviewer: if more times, ask about last time this ever happened).
21c. **The last time, did this theft happen near your own home, elsewhere in your town or city or local area, elsewhere in the country or abroad?**
    O   near own home
    O   elsewhere in the city or local area
    O   elsewhere in the country
    O   abroad
    O   don't know

21d. **The last time, were you holding or carrying what was stolen (e.g. was it a case of pickpocketing?)**
    O   yes
    O   no
    O   don't know

21e. **The last time, what do you estimate roughly the value of the stolen goods to be?**
    (Interviewer: rough estimate)

21f. **Did you or anyone else report the last incident to the police?**
    O   yes
    O   no
    O   don't know

21g. *If not*, **why didn't you report it?**
   (Interviewer: multiple responses allowed).
   If no clear answer: **can you tell me a little more?**
   O not serious enough/no loss/kid's stuff
   O solved it myself/perpetrator known to me
   O inappropriate for police/police not necessary
   O reported to other authorities instead
   O no insurance
   O police could do nothing/lack of proof
   O police won't do anything about it
   O fear/dislike of the police/no involvement wanted with police
   O didn't dare (for fear of reprisal)
   O other reasons
   O don't know

22a. **You mentioned that you had been a victim of a sexual offence. Could I ask you a little about this, like when it happened. Was it then in 1988?**
   If no, **was it before 1988 or was it in 1989?**
   (Interviewer: if respondent has been a victim more than once, ask if this happened at least one time in 1988)
   O yes, in 1988 (at least one time)
   O no, only before 1988
   O no, only in 1989
   O don't know

22b. *If 1988*, **how often did it happen in 1988?**
   O once
   O twice
   O three times
   O four times
   O five times or more
   O don't know

22c. **About the last incident, did you know the offender(s) before the last incident by name or by sight?**
   (Interviewer: if several offenders, count as known, if at least one known)
   O did not know offender(s)
   O known by sight only
   O known by name

22d. **Was it your (ex-)partner, a relative or a close friend?**
   O partner of ex-partner/boyfriend or ex-boyfriend
   O relative
   O close friend
   O none of these
   O refuses to say

22e. **Would you describe the incident as a rape, an attempted rape, an indecent assault or as just behavior which you found offensive?**
   O a rape
   O an attempted rape
   O an indecent behaviour
   O don't know

22f. **Did you or anyone else report that incident to the police?**
   O yes
   O no
   O don't know

164

22g. *If not*, **why didn't you report it?**
(Interviewer: multiple responses allowed).
If no clear answer: **can you tell me a little more?**
O not serious enough/no loss/kid's stuff
O solved it myself/perpetrator known to me
O inappropriate for police/police not necessary
O reported to other authorities instead
O no insurance
O police could do nothing/lack of proof
O police won't do anything about it
O fear/dislike of the police/no involvement wanted with police
O didn't dare (for fear of reprisal)
O other reasons
O don't know

23a. **The attack or threat that you mentioned, when did this happen, was it in 1988?**
If no, **was it before 1988 or was it in 1989?**
(Interviewer: if respondent has been a victim more than once, ask if this happened at least one time in 1988).
O yes, in 1988 (at least one time)
O no, only before 1988
O no, only in 1989
O don't know

23b. *If 1988,* **how often did it happen in 1988?**
O once
O twice
O three times
O four times
O five times or more
O don't know

23c. **The last time, did you know the offender(s) before the incident by name or sight?**
(Interviewer: if several offenders, count as known, if at least one is known).
O did not no offender(s)
O known by sight only
O known by name

23d. **Was it a family member, or someone you have (or had) a close relationship with?**
O yes, family member
O yes, close relationship
O no

23e. **Can you tell me what happened, were you just threatened, or was force actually used?**
O threatened
O force used
O don't know

23f. **Were you grabbed, were you hit, or were you shot, stabbed or assaulted with a weapon?**
O grabbed
O hit
O shot, stabbed, assaulted with weapon
O don't know

23g. **Did your suffer any injury as a result?**
O yes
O no
O don't know

23h. **Did you see a doctor as a result?**
- O yes
- O no
- O don't know

23i. **Did you or anyone else report that last incident to the police?**
- O yes
- O no
- O don't know

23j. *If not,* **why didn't you report it?**
(Interviewer: multiple responses allowed).
If no clear answer: **can you tell me a little more?**
- O not serious enough/no loss/kid's stuff
- O solved it myself/perpetrator known to me
- O inappropriate for police/police not necessary
- O reported to other authorities instead
- O no insurance
- O police could do nothing/lack of proof
- O police won't do anything about it
- O fear/dislike of the police/no involvement wanted with police
- O didn't dare (for fear of reprisal)
- O other reasons
- O don't know

Now I would like to know your opinion about crime in your area.

24. **Please try to remember the last time you went out after dark in your area for whatever reason. Did you stay away from certain streets or areas to avoid crime?**
- O yes
- O no
- O don't know/can't remember
- O never go out

25. **The last time you went out, did you go with someone else to avoid crime?**
- O yes
- O no
- O don't know/can't remember
- O never go out

26. **What would you say are the chances that over the next twelve months someone will try to break into your home? Do you think this is very likely, likely or not likely?**
- O very likely
- O likely
- O not likely
- O don't know

27a. *(Victims 1988 only).* **You told me that you and/or your household have been the victim of one or more crimes last year. In some cities agencies have been set up which help victims of crime by giving information, or practical or emotional support. Have you been helped by such an agency last year?**
- O yes
- O no
- O don't know

166

27b. *If no or don't know*, **looking back at your experiences as a victim (the last time), do you feel the services of such an agency would have been useful for you?**
- O no, not useful
- O yes, useful
- O don't know

28a. *Victims 1988 who reported to the police only.* **As you told me, you or someone else, have reported one or more crimes to the police last year. What has been the last offense you or they reported to the police.**
- O theft of a car
- O theft from a car
- O damage to a car (vandalism)
- O theft of a moped/scooter/motorcycle
- O theft of a bicycle
- O burglary
- O theft involving force
- O theft of personal property
- O sexual offence
- O attack or threat
- O don't know

28b. **The last time, were you or were they satisfied with the way the police dealt with your report or reports?**
- O yes (satisfied)
- O no (dissatisfied)
- O don't know

28c. **Were you very satisfied or just fairly satisfied?**
- O very satisfied
- O satisfied
- O don't know

28d. **Were you somewhat dissatisfied or very dissatisfied?**
- O dissatisfied
- O very dissatisfied
- O don't know

28e. **For what reasons were you dissatisfied? You can give more than one reason.**
- O didn't do enough
- O were not interested
- O didn't find or apprehend the offender
- O didn't recover my property (goods)
- O didn't keep me properly informed
- O didn't treat me correctly/were impolite
- O were slow to arrive
- O other reasons
- O don't know

29a. *(All respondents).* **Taking everything into account, how good do you think the police in your area are in controlling crime? Do you think they do a good job or not?**
- O good job
- O not good job
- O don't know

29b. **Would you say a very good job, or a fairly good job?**
- O very good
- O fairly good
- O don't know

167

29c. **Would you say really bad, or fairly bad?**
   O really bad
   O fairly bad
   O don't know

30a. **People have different ideas about the sentences which should be given to offenders. Take for instance the case of a man of 21 years old who is found guilty of burglary for the second time. The last time he has stolen a colour tv. Which of the following sentences do you consider the most appropriate for such a case.**
   (Interviewer: read out, repeat if necessary)
   O fine
   O prison
   O community service
   O suspended sentence
   O any other sentence
   O does not know *(do not read out)*

30b. **For how long do you think he should go to prison?**
   O 1 month or less
   O 2 months
   O 3 months
   O 4 months
   O 5 months
   O 6 months
   O 7 months
   O 8 months
   O 9 months
   O 10 months
   O 11 months
   O 1 year
   O 2 years
   O 3 years
   O 4 years
   O 5 years
   O 6-10 years
   O 11-15 years
   O 16-20 years
   O 21-25 years
   O more than 25 years
   O life sentence
   O don't know

To analyse the results we want to look at different types of households. To help us can you finally give us a little information about yourself and your household?

31. **First, is the place you are living in now a flat/apartment/maisonette, a terraced home or a detached or semi-detached house?**
   O flat/apartment/maisonette
   O a terraced house/row house
   O detached/semi-detached house
   O boat/caravan/other
   O institution (hospital, house for the elderly)
   O don't know

32. **Does the building you live in, have a caretaker who keeps an eye on things?**
   O yes
   O no
   O don't know

33. **Is your own house protected by a burglar alarm?** *(Interviewer: assure respondent that these data will be treated confidentially and anonymously).*
   O yes
   O no
   O refused
   O don't know

34. **Do you own your house or do you rent?**
   O house is owned
   O house is rented
   O other
   O don't know

35a. **Do you ever keep the lights on when your house/flat/apartment/room is left empty in the evening?**
   (Interviewer: remember the whole interview is confidential)
   O yes
   O no
   O don't know

35b. **Do you do this always or just sometimes?**
   O always
   O sometimes
   O don't know

36. **The last time when no one was home for a day or two, did you ask the neighbour or the caretaker to watch your home?**
   O yes
   O no, neighbours watch anyday
   O no
   O don't know

37a. **Do you or someone else in your household own a gun? By gun I do not mean an air rifle.**
   O yes
   O no
   O don't know
   O refused to say (Northern Ireland only)

37b. *If yes,* **is it a handgun or is it a rifle or shotgun?**
   O handgun
   O rifle/shotgun
   O both
   O don't know

(37c. *For Switzerland,* **is this a private or an army gun, or both?**)

38. **Is your house insurance against burglary?**
   O yes
   O no
   O don't know

39. **How often do you personally go out in the evening for recreational purposes, for instance to go to a pub, restaurant, cinema or to see friends? Is this almost every day, at least once a week, at least once a month or less?**
   O almost every day
   O at least once a week
   O at least once a month
   O less
   O never

169

O don't know

40. **How old were you when you completed your full time education at school, college or elsewhere?**
O still at school   O 20
O < 15   O 21
O 15   O 22
O 16   O 23
O 17   O 24
O 18   O 25 and over
O 19   O don't know

41a. *If not at school,* **do you at the moment have a paid job?**
O yes
O no
O don't know

41b. *If yes,* **is this a part time or full time job?**
O full time
O part time
O part time

42a. **I will now read out some income levels. Please tell me whether your household's combined monthly income after deductions for tax etc. is below or above (median income).**
(Interviewer: take into account the net income, ie, the amount people get on their paycheck).
O below
O above
O don't know

42b. **Is it higher or lower than (bottom 25% limit)?**
O higher
O lower
O don't know

43. **May I ask you your age?**
0 16-19 years
0 20-24
0 25-29
0 30-34
0 35-39
0 40-44
0 45-49
0 50-54
0 55-59
0 60-64
0 65-69
0 70 years or more
0 refused to say

44. **How many people live in your village or town or city?**
(Interviewer: see paper list for guidance).
0 < 10,000 inhabitants
0 10,000 - 50,000
0 50,000 - 100,000
0 100,000 - 500,000
0 500,000 - 1,000,000
0 > 1,000,000 inhabitants
0 don't know

170

Thank you very much for you co-operation in this survey. We realise that we have been asking you some difficult questions. So if you like, I can give you a free telephone number to ring to check that we are a reputable market research company.

(Interviewer: note down your sex).

0 male

0 female

Annex E   Additional tables

Table E.1: Prevalence victimization rates, by country and offence type. Percentage victimized in 1988

	Total[1]	Europe[2]	England & Wales	Scotland	Northern Ireland	Netherlands	West Germany	Switzerland	Belgium	France	Spain	Norway	Finland	USA	Canada	Australia	Warsaw	Surabaja
Theft of car	1.2	1.3	1.8	0.8	1.6	0.3	0.4	0.0	0.8	2.3	1.3	1.1	0.4	2.1	0.8	2.3	2.2	0.2
Theft from car	5.3	5.8	5.6	5.3	4.0	5.3	4.7	1.9	2.7	6.0	9.9	2.8	2.7	9.3	7.2	6.9	10.2	4.7
Car vandalism	6.7	7.0	6.8	6.5	4.5	8.2	8.7	4.1	6.6	6.5	6.3	4.6	4.0	8.9	9.8	8.7	7.6	2.7
Theft of motorcycle[3]	0.4	0.4	0.0	0.3	0.2	0.4	0.2	1.2	0.3	0.6	0.8	0.3	0.0	0.2	0.3	0.2	0.0	0.8
Theft of bicycle	2.6	2.2	1.0	1.0	1.6	7.6	3.3	3.2	2.7	1.4	1.0	2.8	3.1	3.1	3.4	1.9	1.0	2.7
Burglary with entry	2.1	1.8	2.1	2.0	1.1	2.4	1.3	1.0	2.3	2.4	1.7	0.8	0.6	3.8	3.0	4.4	2.6	3.8
Attempted burglary	2.0	1.9	1.7	2.1	0.9	2.6	1.8	0.2	2.3	2.3	1.9	0.4	0.4	5.4	2.7	3.8	2.8	1.7
Robbery	0.9	1.0	0.7	0.5	0.5	0.9	0.8	0.5	1.0	0.4	1.9	0.5	0.8	1.9	1.1	0.9	1.2	0.5
Personal theft	4.0	3.9	3.1	2.6	2.2	4.5	3.9	4.5	4.0	3.6	2.8	3.2	4.3	4.5	5.4	5.0	13.4	5.2
- pickpocketing	1.5	1.8	1.5	1.0	0.9	1.9	1.5	1.7	1.6	2.0	5.0	0.5	1.5	1.3	1.3	1.0	13.0	3.3
Sexual incidents[4]	2.5	1.9	1.2	1.2	1.8	2.6	2.8	1.6	1.3	1.2	2.4	2.1	0.6	4.5	4.0	7.3	3.6	6.3
- sexual assault	0.8	0.7	0.1	0.7	0.5	0.5	1.5	0.0	0.6	0.5	0.7	0.6	0.2	2.3	1.7	1.6	2.0	1.7
Assault/threat	2.9	2.5	1.9	1.8	1.8	3.4	3.1	1.2	2.0	2.0	3.0	3.0	2.9	5.4	4.0	5.2	3.0	0.8
- with force	1.5	1.2	0.6	1.0	1.1	2.0	1.5	0.9	0.7	1.2	1.2	1.4	2.0	2.3	1.5	3.0	1.4	0.3
All crimes[5]	21.1	20.9	19.4	18.6	15.0	26.8	21.9	15.6	17.7	19.4	24.6	16.5	15.9	28.8	28.1	27.8	34.4	20.0

1. Total figure treats each country as of equal statistical importance, with an assumed sample of 2000
2. European totals have been calculated by weighting individual country results by population size
3. 'Motorcycles' include mopeds and scooters
4. Asked of women only
5. Percentage of sample victimized by at least one crime of any type

174

Table E.2: Prevalence victimization rates, by country and offence type. Percentage victimized in past five years *

	Total[1]	Europe[2]	England & Wales	Scotland	Northern Ireland	Nether- lands	West Germany	Switzer- land	Belgium	France	Spain	Norway	Finland	USA	Canada	Australia	Warsaw	Surabaja
Theft of car	4.2	4.6	6.6	5.3	5.2	1.8	1.9	0.9	4.0	7.3	5.0	2.7	1.7	6.3	2.8	8.0	4.6	0.3
Theft from car	14.8	16.6	13.4	12.9	8.5	15.2	14.8	8.4	8.7	21.0	24.6	9.0	8.2	26.7	18.5	17.2	19.8	11.0
Car vandalism	16.9	18.6	17.3	14.9	10.3	21.6	22.1	13.4	17.9	19.6	16.0	11.2	10.5	21.7	18.8	20.8	16.0	5.7
Theft of motorcycle[3]	1.2	1.5	0.4	0.4	0.4	1.3	0.9	4.1	1.4	2.9	2.3	0.6	0.2	0.5	0.6	0.5	0.0	2.8
Theft of bicycle	9.6	8.5	3.9	3.1	4.0	24.8	12.4	12.8	9.8	6.6	3.3	12.5	14.1	9.4	12.4	5.8	4.6	11.0
Burglary with entry	7.8	7.3	9.4	9.0	4.7	8.9	4.7	4.0	7.7	10.4	5.6	3.2	2.0	13.7	10.2	16.6	9.0	11.5
Attempted burglary	6.6	6.6	6.0	5.8	2.9	9.3	5.6	2.1	8.2	8.9	6.9	2.3	2.2	13.5	7.9	11.6	10.8	5.2
Robbery	3.1	3.6	1.9	1.8	1.5	2.0	3.0	2.2	4.0	2.9	9.1	1.5	2.7	5.5	2.6	2.3	4.6	2.8
Personal theft	11.9	12.0	8.3	6.7	6.1	14.3	13.3	15.9	14.9	12.8	13.4	8.3	10.3	14.2	13.2	14.6	27.0	16.0
Sexual incidents[4]	6.3	5.6	3.4	2.9	3.3	6.4	7.9	5.5	4.9	4.3	6.8	4.7	4.3	10.4	10.0	13.5	7.2	14.3
Assault/threat	7.8	7.4	5.3	5.3	4.3	9.3	9.3	3.9	6.4	7.1	7.5	8.2	9.7	12.7	8.8	11.6	7.4	4.2
All crimes[5]	48.4	49.9	46.0	41.4	33.4	60.4	51.3	47.1	48.3	52.0	51.6	38.9	40.1	57.6	53.0	57.2	59.4	44.5

1. Total figure treat each country as of equal statistical importance, with an assumed sample of 2000
2. European totals have been calculated by weighting individual country results by population size
3. 'Motorcycles' include mopeds and scooters
4. Asked of women only
5. Percentage of sample victimized by at least one crime of any type

175

Table E.3: Incidence victimization rates, by country and offence type. Number of offences per 100 population, 1988

	England & Wales	Scotland	Northern Ireland	Netherlands	West Germany	Switzer-land	Belgium	France	Spain	Norway	Finland	USA	Canada	Australia
Theft of car	1.9	0.8	2.0	0.4	0.5	0.0	1.2	2.3	1.8	1.1	0.4	3.0	0.9	3.0
Theft from car	6.5	7.7	4.7	6.9	5.6	2.1	3.5	7.5	14.3	4.0	3.2	12.4	9.0	9.3
Car vandalism	8.7	8.9	6.3	10.9	12.4	4.8	8.7	7.6	9.1	6.2	4.9	12.2	11.6	11.8
Theft of motorcycle	0.1	0.4	0.2	0.4	0.2	1.7	0.5	0.7	1.0	0.5	0.0	0.2	0.3	0.4
Theft of bicycle	1.5	1.4	1.9	10.4	3.8	4.0	3.6	1.5	1.2	2.8	3.8	3.9	4.0	2.3
Burglary with entry[1]	2.2	2.3	1.3	2.6	1.4	1.1	2.8	3.3	2.2	0.9	0.5	5.5	3.7	5.7
Robbery	0.7	0.6	0.5	1.3	1.1	0.5	1.4	0.6	3.9	1.0	0.8	3.0	1.6	1.1
Personal theft	4.0	2.8	3.1	5.1	5.0	5.6	4.2	4.0	6.1	3.3	4.7	6.2	6.6	6.4
Sexual incidents[2]	1.3	2.4	3.7	4.9	5.5	3.2	2.2	1.8	3.3	3.3	0.6	10.9	7.0	18.6
Assault/threat	2.5	3.2	2.7	6.5	4.7	1.6	3.2	3.0	6.2	6.1	3.3	10.1	6.7	9.4

1. Incidence rates for attempted burglary are not available
2. Based on women only

Table E.4: Percentage of incidents reported to the police, by country and offence type, experienced in 1988 and in past five years[1]

1988	Total	Europe	England & Wales	Scotland	Northern Ireland	Nether-lands	West Germany	Switzer-land	Belgium	France	Spain	Norway	Finland	USA	Canada	Australia	Warsaw	Surabaja
Theft of car	93.2	94.6	100.0	100.0	96.9	100.0	95.7	-	88.2	97.1	76.9	81.8	100.0	97.6	82.4	91.3		
Theft from car	62.2	63.6	72.6	79.4	50.0	74.3	79.4	73.7	75.0	71.1	34.0	67.9	71.4	54.6	61.1	57.6		
Car vandalism	38.6	37.2	33.1	51.5	31.5	35.4	39.7	46.3	34.8	48.5	20.3	34.8	36.6	49.2	44.8	27.3		
Theft of motorcycle	85.4	76.9	100.0	66.7	100.0	100.0	90.0	100.0	100.0	88.9	41.2	66.7	-	100.0	100.0	100.0		
Theft of bicycle	60.5	57.6	70.0	65.0	45.2	59.6	66.9	87.5	60.7	28.6	23.8	50.0	56.3	62.3	60.6	74.4		
Burglary with entry	76.9	73.5	88.1	92.7	63.6	93.6	75.0	80.0	72.3	75.0	28.6	75.0	33.3	78.9	80.6	79.5		
Robbery	49.0	45.0	71.4	54.5	80.0	64.7	54.5	46.7	33.3	83.3	22.4	60.0	12.5	59.5	56.5	55.6		
Personal theft	40.7	44.8	55.6	43.4	20.9	41.6	36.1	0.0	43.9	48.1	46.1	25.0	43.2	38.9	29.2	45.0		
Sexual incidents	9.9	8.1	8.3	41.7	10.5	19.2	8.8	0.0	14.3	0.0	4.0	9.1	0.0	12.8	9.3	5.4		
Assault/threat	30.7	29.9	47.4	33.3	50.0	31.3	14.3	25.0	19.0	53.3	24.2	26.7	10.0	34.3	31.7	35.6		
All crimes	49.6	50.0	58.8	62.3	45.8	52.6	47.9	58.7	48.6	60.2	31.5	42.6	41.8	52.1	48.3	46.9		

Past five years	Total	Europe	England & Wales	Scotland	Northern Ireland	Nether-lands	West Germany[2]	Switzer-land	Belgium	France	Spain	Norway	Finland	USA	Canada	Australia	Warsaw	Surabaja
Theft of car	90.2	91.2	95.5	91.5	96.1	91.4	89.0	88.9	85.5	95.4	77.7	74.1	64.7	97.6	87.9	90.7	87.0	100.0
Theft from car	61.6	62.0	69.8	78.4	55.3	72.4	82.7	71.4	65.0	68.4	31.8	58.2	60.7	60.0	64.3	54.8	68.7	19.7
Car vandalism	40.0	37.9	31.9	49.7	36.1	35.7	46.2	47.0	37.4	47.3	21.8	37.2	42.6	55.6	48.2	25.4	18.8	2.9
Theft of motorcycle	82.4	76.4	87.5	88.9	87.5	96.0	91.8	87.8	92.9	83.7	47.8	83.3	100.0	77.8	100.0	90.9	90.9	35.3
Theft of bicycle	66.6	65.9	75.6	77.8	57.5	73.2	73.6	84.4	70.3	54.5	26.9	45.2	63.4	63.1	69.6	69.8	34.8	16.7
Burglary with entry	82.4	81.4	90.4	92.8	85.1	93.8	99.2	80.0	78.5	84.0	47.4	78.1	60.0	79.9	83.0	84.4	82.2	18.8
Robbery	45.3	42.4	68.4	48.6	60.0	52.5	48.1	40.9	41.5	50.0	29.6	33.3	32.1	58.2	57.4	53.2	34.8	29.4
Personal theft	43.8	47.9	59.0	51.1	25.4	48.1	39.7	42.1	50.2	52.8	42.5	31.0	37.7	41.0	38.1	45.1	23.7	19.8
Sexual incidents	12.0	11.0	11.4	30.0	8.8	12.3	12.6	21.4	15.4	15.2	4.2	4.2	8.7	18.5	10.2	7.2	0.0	0.0
Assault/threat	34.7	32.6	43.9	43.4	51.8	38.9	26.1	25.6	35.9	36.8	27.9	28.9	18.2	41.7	38.5	35.6	21.6	24.0
All crimes	53.8	53.7	61.1	66.5	53.3	58.6	55.9	58.3	54.1	60.9	33.7	42.9	44.8	57.5	55.4	50.7	40.6	17.5

1) Based on last incident of the type mentioned
2) Estimated on the basis of the data about 1988 and limited data about previous years

177

Table E.5: Prevalence victimization rates, by country and offence type. Percentage victimized in 1988 and in past five years

1988	Total Europe	England & Wales	Scotland	Northern Ireland	Nether-lands	West Germany	Switzer-land	Belgium	France	Spain	Norway	Finland	USA	Canada	Australia	Warsaw	Surabaja
Property crime[1]	15.4	15.3	14.1	13.5	11.1	20.5	16.5	12.0	12.8	14.2	16.9	12.3	12.0	19.9	20.9	18.8	18.4	11.7
Burglary[2]	3.6	3.3	3.5	3.9	1.8	4.7	2.7	1.1	3.5	4.7	3.3	1.0	0.8	7.5	5.3	7.3	5.2	4.3
Contact crime[3]	5.5	5.4	4.2	3.1	3.6	6.1	6.0	3.9	4.6	3.0	8.4	4.8	4.8	8.3	6.9	8.6	18.2	7.5

5 years	Total Europe	England & Wales	Scotland	Northern Ireland	Nether-lands	West Germany	Switzer-land	Belgium	France	Spain	Norway	Finland	USA	Canada	Australia	Warsaw	Surabaja
Property crime[1]	37.8	39.1	33.7	30.7	24.4	50.4	42.6	37.2	36.6	40.5	38.8	31.0	31.3	46.3	43.2	43.0	36.0	30.0
Burglary[2]	12.3	12.1	13.6	13.1	6.9	15.9	8.8	5.6	12.7	16.6	10.9	4.8	3.7	21.6	15.5	23.3	18.0	15.0
Contact crime[3]	14.7	15.0	10.9	9.3	8.8	16.0	15.7	13.4	15.2	15.6	20.1	12.9	15.3	19.3	14.5	18.7	33.8	28.2

1. Property crime: theft of cars, motorcycles, bicycles; theft from cars, car vandalism; other personal theft (excluding pickpocketing)
2. Burglary; including attempts
3. Contact crimes: pickpocketing; robbery; sexual incidents and threat or assault

Table E.6: Overall national victimization rates (percentages victimized in 1988), and percentage of population living in cities of more than 100,000 residents

	overall victimization risk, 1988	% living in cites of more than 100,000 residents
Total	21.1	23.0
Europe	20.9	27.1
England & Wales	19.4	32.2
Scotland	18.6	•23.4
N.Ireland	15.0	1.6
Netherlands	26.8	18.5
W.Germany	21.9	26.3
Switzerland	15.6	10.1
Belgium	17.7	5.9
France	19.4	20.4
Spain	24.6	44.7
Norway	16.5	16.3
Finland	15.9	22.1
USA	28.8	19.6
Canada	28.1	45.4
Australia	27.8	34.8

Table E.7: Vehicle incidence victimization rates for vehicle offences, 1988. Number of offences per 100 vehicles owned

	Theft of cars	Theft from cars	Car vandalism	Motorcycle theft	Bicycle theft
Total	1.2	5.8	8.5	3.2	2.4
Europe	1.3	7.0	8.9	3.0	2.2
England & Wales	1.9	6.3	8.3	0.6	2.3
Scotland	0.9	9.1	10.5	8.2	2.5
N.Ireland	2.0	4.9	6.5	3.3	2.0
Netherlands	0.4	7.6	12.0	2.8	4.2
W.Germany	0.4	4.9	10.9	1.9	2.1
Switzerland	0.0	2.2	5.0	5.6	2.6
Belgium	1.1	3.2	8.2	3.4	2.8
France	1.9	6.2	6.2	3.4	1.3
Spain	2.1	17.1	10.9	4.0	2.0
Norway	1.0	3.5	5.5	4.7	1.9
Finland	0.4	3.3	5.0	0.0	1.8
USA	1.4	5.8	5.7	0.7	2.5
Canada	0.6	5.8	7.4	2.6	2.5
Australia	1.9	6.0	7.7	3.0	2.4

Table E.8: Victimization rates for vehicle crimes. Percentages of owners victimized in past five years

	Theft of cars	Theft from cars	Car vandalism	Motorcycle theft	Bicycle theft
Total	5.3	18.5	21.1	9.8	16.1
Europe	5.9	21.2	23.8	11.6	14.8
England & Wales	8.6	17.3	22.5	6.2	10.8
Scotland	7.6	18.7	21.6	10.7	10.1
N.Ireland	7.1	11.7	14.1	9.9	9.0
Netherlands	2.3	19.7	27.9	9.8	27.3
W.Germany	2.4	18.4	27.4	8.6	16.3
Switzerland	1.1	10.7	17.1	16.4	18.5
Belgium	4.9	10.7	21.9	11.5	16.7
France	8.6	24.9	23.2	17.3	11.8
Spain	7.4	36.3	23.5	10.6	8.3
Norway	3.3	11.3	14.0	6.1	17.2
Finland	2.2	10.6	13.7	1.8	16.0
USA	6.6	27.9	22.7	3.1	14.2
Canada	3.2	20.8	21.2	5.8	19.5
Australia	9.0	19.5	23.4	5.7	12.0

Table E.9: Survey measure of (i) assaults/threats; (ii) sexual offences; and (iii) robbery (percentage victim in past five years), compared to offences recorded by the police, 1982-1986, offences per 100,000 population[1]

	Assaults/threats		Sexual offences		Robbery	
	survey	police[2]	survey[3]	police[4]	survey	police[5]
England & Wales	5.3	228	3.4	42	1.9	51
Scotland	5.3	106	2.9	104	1.8	85
N.Ireland	4.3	141	3.3	37	1.5	126
Netherlands	9.3	112	6.4	61	2.0	54
W.Germany	9.3	106	7.9	66	3.0	48
Switzerland	3.9	47	5.5	53	2.2	22
Belgium	6.4	84	4.9	41	4.0	54
France	7.1	70	4.3	33	2.9	100
Spain	7.5	24	6.8	12	9.1	132
Norway	8.2	23	4.7	23	1.5	15
Finland	9.7	37	4.3	31	2.7	36
USA	12.7	302	10.4	n/a	5.5	217
Canada	8.8	121	10.0	70	2.6	96
Australia	11.6	63	13.5	79	2.3	73

1) Source: Interpol returns 1982-1986, augmented by additional national statistics. Number of offences per 100,000 population.
2) Interpol returns, category 3.
3) Question asked of women only. Risks to women only, sexual assaults and offensive behaviour. % victimized once or more in past five years.
4) Interpol returns, category 2.
5) Interpol returns, category 4.1.1.

Table E.10: Survey measure of (i) burglary; (ii) theft of vehicles (percentage victim in past five years), compared to offences recorded by the police, 1982-1986, offences per 100,000 population[1]

	Burglary survey[2]	police[3]	Theft of vehicles survey	police[4]
England & Wales	9.4	1742	6.6	724
Scotland	9.0	2039	5.3	596
N.Ireland	4.7	1325	5.2	420
Netherlands	8.9	2241	1.8	151
W.Germany	4.7	1634	1.9	121
Switzerland	4.0	1041	0.9	n/a
Belgium	7.7	652	4.0	150
France	10.4	772	7.3	484
Spain	5.6	1138	5.0	278
Norway	3.2	123	2.7	463
Finland	2.0	821	1.7	182
USA	13.7	1342	6.3	459
Canada	10.2	1442	2.8	324
Australia	16.6	1714	8.0	637

1) Source: Interpol returns 1982-1986, augmented by additional national statistics. Number of offences per 100,000 population.
2) Burglary excluding attempts. % victimized once or more in past five years.
3) Interpol returns, category 4.1.2.
4) Interpol returns, category 4.2

Table E.11: Rank order correlation between survey measures of victimization and offences recorded by the police[1]

	rank order correlations
Theft of vehicles[2]	
unadjusted	.786
adjusted for 'own country'[3]	.813
adjusted for reporting[4]	.714
Burglary[5]	
burglary/entry, unadjusted	.442
burglary/entry + attempts, unadjusted	.490
burglary/entry, adjusted for reporting	.473
Robbery	
unadjusted	.371
adjusted for 'own country'	.618
adjusted for reporting	.666
Assaults[6]	
assaults/threats, unadjusted	.037
assaults/force, unadjusted	-.178
assaults/threats, adjusted for reporting	.653
Sexual offences[7]	
sexual incidents, unadjusted	.247
sexual assaults, unadjusted	.396
sexual incidents, adjusted for reporting	.835

1) Police figures are based on crimes per 100,000 population (all ages); survey figures are based on 5-year prevalence rates (those aged 16 or more). Annual returns are often not made to Interpol. Additional crime figures were collected from other sources where possible.
2) Survey figures exclude motorbikes and bicycles. Interpol figures are often for undefined vehicles. Switzerland is excluded.
3) Excluding from survey figures incidents which were said to have happened abroad, based on the 'last incident' of the offence type which occurred over the 5-year period.
4) Figures of percentage of incidents said to have been reported to the police are taken, based on the 'last incident' of the offence type which occurred over the 5-year period.
5) Interpol figures include all burglaries (residential and commercial).
6) Percentage of assaults with force based on 1988 data.
7) USA excluded because of missing police data. Survey risks based on women only. Percentage of sexual assaults based on 1988 data.

References

BIENKOVSKA, E. (1989). 'Crime control and penal reform in Poland'. *Justitiële Verkenningen*, Special Issue: Perestrojka and Penal Law. Research and Documentation Centre, Ministry of Justice, Vol. 15, May 1989 (in Dutch).

BILES, D. and HILL, L. (1987). 'Statistics, Asian and Pacific Series'. *Reporter*, Vol. 8, No. 2, June 1987.

BLOCK, R.L. (Ed.) (1984a). *Victimization and Fear of Crime: World Perspectives*. Bureau of Justice Statistics: US Department of Justice. Washington, DC: Government Printing Office.

BLOCK, R.L. (1984b). 'The impact of victimization and patterns: a comparison of the Netherlands and the United States'. In, BLOCK, R.L. (Ed.), *Victimization and Fear of Crime: World Perspectives*. Bureau of Justice Statistics: US Department of Justice. Washington, DC: Government Printing Office.

BLOCK, R.L. (1987). *A comparison of victimization, crime assessment, and fear of crime in England & Wales, the Netherlands, Scotland, and the United States*. Paper presented to the Council of Europe Conference on the Reduction of Urban Insecurity, Barcelona, Spain, 1987.

BOERS, K. and SESSAR, K. (1988). *Do people really want punishment? On the relationship between acceptance of restitution, needs for punishment and fear of crime*. Paper presented to 10th International Congress of Criminology, 4-9 September, Hamburg, 1988.

BRILLON, Y. (1988). Punitiveness, status and ideology in three Canadian provinces. In, WALKER, N. and HOUGH, M. (eds.), *Public Attitudes to Sentencing*, Aldershot/Gower, 1988.

CATLIN, G. and MURRAY, S. (1979). *Report on the Canadian Victimization Survey Methodological Pretests*. Ottawa: Statistics Canada.

COHEN, L.E. and FELSON, N. 'Social change and crime rate trends. A routine activities approach'. *American Sociological Review*, 44, 588-607.

COHEN, L.E. and LAND, K.C. (1984). 'Discrepancies between crime reports and crime surveys: urban and structural determinants'. *Criminology*, 22, 499-530.

COHEN, L. and LICHBACH, M.I. (1982). 'Alternative measures of crime: a statistical evaluation'. *The Sociological Quarterly*, 23, 253-266.

COLLINS, M., SYKES, W., WILSON, P. and BLACKSHAW, N. (1988). 'Nonresponse: the UK experience'. In, GROVES, R.M., BIEMER, P., LYBERG, L. NICHOLLS, W.L. and WAKSBERG, J. *Telephone Survey Methodology*: New York: John Wiley.

Van DIJK, J.J.M. (1986). Responding to Crime: reflections on the reactions of victims and non-victims to the increase in petty crime. In, FATTAH, E. (ed.), *Reorienting the Justice System: from crime policy to victim policy.* London, Macmillan, 1986.

Van DIJK, J.J.M., LEGER, G.J. and SHAPLAND, J. (1987). *Information systems, crime and crime prevention.* Paper presented to the Council of Europe Conference on the Reduction of Urban Insecurity, Barcelona, Spain, 1987.

Van DIJK, J.J.M. and STEINMETZ, C.H.D. (1983). 'Victimization surveys: beyond measuring the volume of crime'. *Victimology: an International Journal,* 8, 291-301.

Van DIJK, J.J.M. and STEINMETZ, C.H.D. (1984). 'The burden of crime in Dutch society, 1973-1979'. In, Block, R.L. (Ed.), *Victimization and Fear of Crime: World Perspectives.* Bureau of Justice Statistics: US Department of Justice, Washington, DC: Government Printing Office.

Van DIJK, J.J.M. and STEINMETZ, C.H.D. (1988). 'Pragmatism, ideology and crime control: three Dutch surveys'. In, N. WALKER en M. HOUGH (Eds.), *Public Attitudes to Sentencing*, Aldershot: Gower.

EIJKEN, A.W.M. (1989). *Criminaliteitsbeeld van Nederland.* Directie Criminaliteitspreventie, Ministerie van Justitie, Den Haag.

EUROMONITOR (1987). *European Marketing Data and Statistics 1987/1988/International Market, Data and Statistics 1987/1988.* Euromonitor Pubications Ltd., London.

FIGGIE REPORT, the, Part VI (1988). *The Business of Crime: the criminal perspective.* Figgie International Inc., Richmond, 1988.

FISELIER, J.P.S. (1978). *Slachtoffers van delicten. Een onderzoek naar verborgen criminaliteit.* Utrecht: Ars Aequi Libri.

GALLUP INTERNATIONAL (1984). *International Crime Study.* Gallup Poll, November, 1984. Poll conducted for the Daily Telegraph.

GOTTFREDSON, M.R. (1986). 'The substantive contribution of victimization survey' In, TONRY, M. H. and MORRIS, N. (Eds.), *Crime and Justice: an annual review of research.* Vol 7. Chicago: University of Chicago Press.

GROVES, R.M. and LYBERG, L. (1988). 'An overview of nonresponse issues in telephone surveys'. In, GROVES, R.M., BIEMER, P., LYBERG, L. NICHOLLS, W.L. and WAKSBERG, J. *Telephone Survey Methodology*: New York: John Wiley.

HESSELING, R. (1989). *Evaluation of Caretakers Program; results of the first survey amongst residents.* Research and Documentation Centre, Ministry of Justice (in Dutch).

HOUGH, M.J. (1984). 'Residential burglary: findings from the British Crime Survey'. In, CLARKE, R.V.G., and HOPE, T. (Eds.), *Coping with Burglary.* Boston, Mass.: Kluwer-Nijhoff.

HOUGH, M.J. (1986). 'Victims of violence crime'. In, FATTAH, E. (Ed.), *Reorienting the Justice System: from crime policy to victim policy.* London: Macmillan.

HOUGH, M.J. and MO. J. (1989). 'If at first you don't succeed: British Crime Survey findings on attempted burglaries'. *Research Bulletin*, No. 21. London: Home Office Research and Planning Unit.

KALISH, C. (1988). *International Crime Rates.* Bureau of Justice Statistics Special Report. US Department of Justice. Washington DC: Government Printing Office.

KILLIAS, M. (1989). *Les Suisses Face au Crime.* Grusch (Switzerland): Ruegger.

KILLIAS, M., KUHN, A. and CHEVALIER, C. (1987). 'Nouvelles perspectives methodologiques en matiere de sondages de victimisation: l'experience de enquetes Suisses'. *Deviance et Societe*, 34-330.

KLECKA, W.R and TUCHFARBER, A.J. (1978). 'Random digit dialling: a comparison to personal surveys'. *Public Opinion Quarterly, 42*, 105-114.

KORTHALS ALTES, H.J. and Van SOOMEREN, P. (1989). *Samenvatting Modus Operandi onderzoek woninginbraken.* Landelijk Bureau Voorkoming Misdrijven, 1989.

MASSEY, J.T. (1988). 'An overview of telephone coverage'. In, GROVES, R.M., BIEMER, P., LYBERG, L. NICHOLLS, W.L. and WAKSBERG, J. *Telephone Survey Methodology*: New York: John Wiley.

MAXFIELD, M.G. (1987). 'Household composition, routine activity, and victimization: a comparative analysis'. *Journal of Quantitative Criminology, 3,* 301-320.

MAYHEW, P., CLARKE, R.V.G, STURMAN, A. and HOUGH, J.M. (1976). *Crime as Opportunity.* Home Office Research Study, No. 34, London: HSMO.

MAYHEW, P. (1987). *Residential Burglary: a comparison of the US, Canada and England & Wales.* National Institute of Justice. Washington, DC: Government Printing Office.

MAYHEW, P. (1985). 'The effects of crime: victims, the public and fear'. In, *Research on Victimisation. Collected Studies in Criminological Research.* Vol. XXII. Strasbourg: Council of Europe.

MAYHEW, P. and SMITH, L.J.F. (1985). 'Crime in England & Wales and Scotland: a British Crime Survey comparison'. *British Journal of Criminology, 25,* 148-159.

MAYHEW, P., CLARKE, R.V.G. and ELLIOTT, D. (1989). 'Motorcycle theft, helmet legislation and displacement'. *The Howard Journal,* 25, 1-8.

McGINN, L. (1989). 'Computer Assisted Telephone Interviewing' In, Saphire, D. (Ed.), *NCS News. Newsletter No. 1 of the National Crime Survey User's Group.* Alexandria, VA: American Statistical Association.

NEUMAN, W.L. and BERGER, R. (1988). 'Competing Perspective on Cross-National Crime; an evaluation of theory and evidence'. *Sociological Quarterly, 29,* 281-313.

REPPETTO, T.A. (1974). *Residential Crime.* Cambridge, Mass.: Ballinger.

ROBERT, Ph. et FAUGERON, C. (1978). *La justice et son public: les représentations sociales du système pénal.* Genève-Paris: Medicine et Hygiène-Masson.

ROMAN, A.M. and SILVA, G.E. (1982). *Results from the examination of the effects of increased telephone usage in the National Crime Survey.* Washington, DC: Bureau of the Census (mimeo).

SAMPSON, R.J. and WOOLDREDGE, J.D. (1987). 'Linking the micro and macro-level dimensions of lifestyle-routine activity and opportunity models of predatory victimization'. *Journal of Quantitative Criminology, 3,* 371-393.

SAMPSON. R.J. (1987). 'Personal violence by strangers: an extension and test of the opportunity model of predatory victimization'. *Journal of Criminal Law and Criminology, 78*, 327-356.

SKOGAN, W.G. (1986). 'Methodological issues in the study of victimisation'. In, E.A. FATTAH (Ed.), *From Crime Policy to Victim Policy*. Basingstoke: Macmillan.

SKOGAN, W.G. (1984). 'Reporting crimes to the police: the status of world research'. *Journal of Research in Crime and Delinquency, 21*, 113-137.

SOURCE, BURKE. (1987). *The European Network*. Amsterdam: Source International (September).

SPARKS, R.F. (1982). *Research on Victims of Crime: accomplishments, issues, and new directions*. Rockville, MD. National Institute Of Mental Health, Centre for Studies of Crime and Delinquency.

SVERI, K. (1982). 'Comparative analyses of crime by means of victim surveys: the Scandinavian experience.' In, SCHNEIDER, H.J. (Ed.), *The Victim in International Perspective*. Papers and essays given at the Third International Symposium on Victimology, Muenster, Westphalia, September, 1979. Berlin and New York: De Gruyter.

TESKE, R. and ARNOLD, H. (1982). 'A comparative investigation of criminal victimization in the United States and the Federal Republic of Germany'. In, KAISER, H. (Ed.), *Research in Criminal Justice. Stocktaking of criminological research at the Max-Planck-Institute for Foreign and International Penal Law after a Decade*. Freiburg i.Br., Max-Planck-Institute.

TORNUDD, P. (1982). *Measuring Victimization: the OECD Special Indicators Development Programme*. Special Study No. 6. Paris: OECD.

TREWIN, D. and LEE, G. (1988). 'International comparisons in telephone coverage'. In, GROVES, R.M., BIEMER, P., LYBERG, L. NICHOLLS, W.L. and WAKSBERG, J. *Telephone Survey Methodology*: New York: John Wiley.

US DEPARTMENT OF COMMERCE. (1989). *Statistical Abstracts of the United States, 1989*, 109th Edition. Bureau of the Census. Washington, DC.: Government Printing Office.

US DEPARTMENT OF JUSTICE. (1988). *Report to the Nation on Crime and Justice*. 2nd Edition. Bureau of Justice Statistics. Washington, DC.: Government Printing Office.

WALKER, N., HOUGH, M. and LEWIS, H. (1988) 'Tolerance of leniency and severity in England and Wales'. In, WALKER, N. HOUGH, M. (Eds.), Public *Attitudes to Sentencing*. Cambridge Studies in Criminology LIX, Aldershot: Gower.

WALLER, I. and OKIHIRO, N. (1978). *Burglary: the victim and the public*. Toronto: University of Toronto Press.

WOLTMAN, H.F., TURNER, A.G., and BUSHERY, J.M. (1980). 'A comparison of three mixed-mode interviewing procedures in the National Crime Survey'. *Journal of the American Statistical Association, 75*, 534-543.

188